As a writer and humorist, Mary Killen made her mark at the *Tatler* with her column 'Candid Counsel', forerunner of *The Spectator*'s 'Dear Mary'. She writes regularly for *Harpers and Queen* and *The Times*, and lives in Wiltshire with her husband and daughter.

MARY KILLEN

Dear Mary

THE *SPECTATOR* BOOK
OF SOLUTIONS

Illustrated by Beatrix Nevill

HarperCollins*Publishers*

HarperCollins*Publishers*
77–85 Fulham Palace Road,
Hammersmith, London W6 8JB

Published by HarperCollins*Publishers* 1993

1 3 5 7 9 8 6 4 2

Copyright © Mary Killen 1993

The Author asserts the moral right to
be identified as the author of this work

A catalogue record for this book is
available from the British Library

ISBN 0 00 255261 2

Set in Linotron Baskerville

Printed and bound in Great Britain by
Butler & Tanner Ltd, Frome and London

Contents

———∽∽———

Ageing Boyfriends

Q I WONDER IF you can solve a predicament which occurred during a recent interlude abroad? A lady hotel guest asked if I was on holiday. I replied that I was, but that it was a business trip for my boyfriend who was with me. As his and my combined ages reach over a century, he found this embarrassing and said I could have used a different way to describe him. Neither of us could think of anything suitable. Lover might have implied I frequently went abroad with sundry men; partner could have referred to a business relationship, and our sharing a room might have indicated the business was doing badly; and husband was out of the question because we talked to each other throughout dinner. Can you give him a suitable title? I would be grateful.

F.B., London

A I RECENTLY looked into this subject in some depth, examining all the descriptive possibilities for 'boyfriends'. I concluded that almost all the options were unacceptable, particularly the word 'partner'. One can joke to friends that one is now 'romantically linked, as they say in the tabloids', but in the scenario you mention you might have described your elderly boyfriend to the lady hotel guest as 'my unofficial fiancé'. A conspiratorial wink enacted as you said these words would have ensured that she did not ask him any embarrassing questions about wedding dates.

Acquiring Charisma

Q THEY SAY that the late Robert Maxwell used to turn heads when he entered a room. I have the same effect but the heads turn away. Is it possible to acquire charisma, to make oneself more interesting? What do you suggest?

T.H., Luton, Beds

A I HAVE NOTED, on the social circuit, that certain people can attain a spurious charisma by wearing a knowing smile on their lips and saying little. Their demeanour serves to unnerve others who presume that there must be more to such a person than meets the eye. Inevitably, this success is short-lived and the practitioner very soon unmasked, unless he is a younger person moving in drug-taking circles and the silences are taken to denote wisdom. Many of the most pointless people of the 1960s and '70s got away with being cyphers for years by using this method. You may, of course, not wish to build your social life around drug-taking. If you are a man, another way of gaining charisma is to make passes at virtually every woman you meet. Englishwomen are so surprised that roughly four out of ten will accept the overture. The confidence which accrues to you as a sequel to such submissions will help to develop any latent charisma you may have.

THE
SILENCE

BY.
TH.
LUTON
BEDS.

BEATRIX NEILL

One final comment: *all* 'Dear Mary' queries are genuine. The vast majority come from strangers, though my own friends do submit queries from time to time.

The identities of those who write are not revealed, for obvious reasons. Douglas Hurd, John Simpson and Nigel Nicolson are exceptions: they contributed to a special 'Christmas Celebrity Problems' column.

Any reader who wishes to inspect my correspondence in order to authenticate my claim may do so but, for ethical reasons, I *must* conceal the identities of the correspondents. They are usually people in prominent positions who would have a lot to lose were their anxieties fully exposed to the public gaze.

Introduction

If you have purchased *Dear Mary: The* Spectator *Book of Solutions*, you may be confident that at the very least your financial outlay will be speedily recouped, since budgetary savings are a by-product of many of my solutions.

Spectator readers as a group tend not to need to consult conventional etiquette guides. In certain couture houses there is a saying, 'If you have to ask how much it is, you can't afford it.' Equally *Spectator* readers take the view that if you need to consult an etiquette book in order to pass yourself off as a gentleman, then there is no chance of your succeeding.

Where the readers do require assistance is in the matter of more sophisticated scenarios. The Foreign Secretary, for example, wrote to me last Christmas with a query about how he should hurry his guests on an RAF plane off to bed without seeming to be a spoil-sport.

What does a world-famous novelist do when he finds himself seated in a restaurant next door to another world-famous novelist who is feeling self-conscious about his ability to overhear her conversation?

These and other queries are answered with unique foolproof solutions.

One field in which I take a particular interest is that of romance and the difficulty of finding a suitable partner in these transient times. Even when that goal is achieved, many of my readers find themselves crippled by shyness once it comes to making the first physical overture. You will find in these pages full step-by-step guides to making ambiguous passes which will assist you in precluding the embarrassment of rejection.

Allergies and Social Problems

Q I HAVE BEEN told by an allergist that I am allergic
to wheat and milk, and I have certainly felt dramatically better since I gave up foodstuffs containing
these products. My problem is that my parents-in-law
clearly think the whole thing is a load of nonsense and
that I am neurotic. Whenever I go to stay with them
they try to press me to have things with wheat or milk
in them, saying, 'Go on, don't be silly. Humans have
been eating wheat and drinking milk since time immem-
orial.' My persistent refusal induces an atmosphere of
tension in the household. What should I do?

Name and address withheld

A COLLUDE WITH your allergist to produce a personalised fact-sheet for you which will detail all those
foodstuffs which you must avoid and the consequences
of your failure to do so. Then pop this fact-sheet into an
envelope. Address it by typewriter to yourself c/o your
parents-in-law. Next time you go to stay with them post
this letter to yourself so that it arrives the day before you
do. Stamp the envelope 'URGENT'. On receipt, one of
your parents-in-law will surely telephone you to advise
you of the arrival of an urgent letter. At this point you
can say, 'I cannot think what it can be. Could you open
it and read it out to me over the phone in case it can't
wait until tomorrow?' No doubt they will be chagrined
by the contents and will be less eager to pressurise you
into consuming debilitating foodstuffs when you arrive
to stay with them on the following day.

Animal 'Lib' Altercations

Q I WAS QUEUING for a ticket at my local station last week, when the man behind me smiled pleasantly and enquired whether I myself had shot the brace of pheasants whose tail-feathers were sticking out of a plastic bag I was carrying. I replied, equally pleasantly, that, no, my husband had shot them. 'He must be a bloody brave man!' the stranger began, before launching into a stream of vicious expletives. Too late did I realise that he was an animal liberationist. How should I avoid exciting verbal and other abuse from such people at this time of year, when I am regularly carrying pheasants up on the train for London friends? They are not exactly easy to disguise.

D.McC., Sheringham, Norfolk

A CONTINUE to carry the pheasants openly but do not truss them together at the necks. If you are approached by threatening strangers you should allow a mournful expression to come over your face, then say, 'Isn't it sad? I found them run over on the road and I thought I'd take them home and give them a decent burial in my garden.'

Annoying Fellow Workers

Q MY CO-WORKER is a continual irritant, staring and looming over me with a daily barrage of criticism, self-puffery, interference and unsolicited advice. Responding increases the verbal flow, while ignoring it offers no respite whatsoever. I'd feel sorry for her – her job is her life – if I didn't feel so victimised myself! Our employer, whose job said co-worker once held on an interim basis, doesn't want to know. My predecessor quit in frustration. Please tell me there's another option.

J.S., sw1

A KEEP A GIANT ledger open on your desk. Then when your co-worker begins her barrage you can say sweetly: 'Oh do please write down your advice. I'm sure to forget it otherwise.'

Antique Dealer's Problem

Q I AM AN ANTIQUE dealer dealing with what we call in the trade *important* furniture. My problem is that my social life is not my own. Whenever I go into anyone's house for drinks, dinner, for whatever social reason they tend to say 'While you're here . . .', and to start showing me pieces of Victoriana worth about £50. How can I politely discourage friends and acquaintances from taking me on guided tours of their houses when I just want to relax?

M.W., W1

A WHY NOT TAKE your cue from one well-known social art dealer who handles this problem in the following way. ' "While you're here," ' he ripostes in genial manner. 'That's going to be the title of my auto-biography!' He then follows his host or hostess pleasantly towards the *objet*, but finds that his remark has discon-certed them sufficiently to preclude his being shown more than one piece of unimportant furniture.

Art Dealer Wishes to Reject Bad Artists Tactfully

Q I AM AN ART dealer who has recently left a West
End gallery in order to deal privately. My problem
is that in my social life I am constantly being asked by
bad artists and the friends of bad artists if I would like
to see their work, sell it, etc. How can I reject them
without incurring their resentment?

Name withheld, SW1

A IF, AS YOU say, you deal privately, it is unlikely
that any of these people you meet socially can be
quite sure of exactly what sort of art you deal in. A
decisive way for you to avoid embarrassment, following
such a proposal, is to allow your face to light up briefly
before you shake your head sadly and say, 'Hmmph. I
don't deal in any living artists, more's the pity.'

Avoiding Buying at a Christmas Sale

Q IN RECENT weeks I have been inundated by a
veritable flood of invitations to 'Christmas Sales'
where wives of Lloyd's names and similar club together
to hold a sale of their wares in a friend's house. Often
the friend will say 'Come and stay to lunch or dinner

afterwards!', but even if they don't, one feels honour-bound to buy something from amongst the selection of costume jewellery, hand-made jumpers, pot-pourri devoid of any smell, wooden ashtrays that catch fire and dried flower decorations. One wouldn't mind, but there is a limit to the number of things one wants for oneself or to give as a present, and I find myself becoming slightly bitter as my cupboard fills up with these unwanted gifts. Yet one cannot leave without saying goodbye and if you try to leave empty-handed they say, 'Surely we can find something for you . . .' and one is virtually forced to buy something.

S.H., Cirencester

A THE BEST solution is to arrive at the sale with a large carrier bag in your hand. Lying on the bottom of the bag should be two unused sheets of tissue paper, slim and smooth and about the size of two airmail letters. Halfway through your tour of the stalls you can pop to the loo and fluff your tissue paper up so that it takes up the whole plastic bag. Drop some coins into the bottom of the bag to give it weight and then return to the mêlée. Carry on chatting your way around the room and being pleasant. You can then look at your watch suddenly and pretend you are late for another appointment. Make hurried goodbyes so that no one has time to ask you exactly what you bought. The important thing is that you will appear to have bought something.

Avoiding Buying the Author's Book at a Book Launch

Q I ALWAYS enjoy attending book launching parties at this time of year but feel that there is currently an increasing pressure on one actually to purchase the book at the launch. It's not that I am mean but I often just don't want the book in question on my shelves. What is the correct way to avoid buying the book without seeming to be rude to the author? You cannot say you already have it as they are not normally in the shops on the night of the launch.

A.B., w8

A IT IS A RELATIVELY easy matter to establish roughly the size and shape of the book being launched before you attend the party. Having done this you need only bring along a plastic or paper bag containing a book of similar dimensions. You can leave this on the floor or on a surface within reach and can pick it up and hold it when you feel the pressure mounting. Your passage out of the party will be considerably eased by being able to carry such a package with you and, of course, there will be no need for you to make reference to what the package contains at any time.

Avoiding Buying Things in Shops

Q IF A SHOP-ASSISTANT goes to any trouble or spends a lot of time with me, I often feel too embarrassed not to buy something at the end of it. I always collapse under pressure when they stand back in silent contempt of one's indecisiveness. How do other people get out of these situations?

A WHY NOT KEEP a cheque book about your person which has just the cover and the stubs but no spare cheques inside? This enables you to put the assistant to as much trouble as you like, secure in the confidence that when all purchase possibilities have been exhausted, you can say, 'That's absolutely lovely, I'll take that,' and then appear to be frustrated by the fact that you have run out of cheques. You can then leave the shop in despair saying ambiguously, 'I'm sure I have another cheque book at home.'

Avoiding Charitable Contributions

Q YOUR SUGGESTED method for dealing with door-
step collectors for charity was clever ('There's no
one in, I'm just cleaning up here') but for my part I find
the entrepreneurial and usually suspect caller at the door
easy to handle. It is the embarrassingly hand-written
genuine appeal from a respected neighbour that has left
me flummoxed. I have no desire to contribute to the
charity she supports, but do not wish to seem to rebuff
her. What should I do?

C.G., Alton, Hants

A WRITE BACK to your neighbour enclosing a nom-
inal sum and a friendly letter explaining that you
have your own pet charity which precludes you from
making substantial donations to any other. You should
keep a stock of relevant leaflets for the charity you have
chosen and enclose one of these in your letter, suggesting
that she too might be interested in helping it. In this way
you may redirect any moral blackmail.

Bird's Nests in the Chimney

Q HOW CAN I check whether or not there is a bird's nest in my chimney? We had it swept very recently but it still seems to be smoking.

L.G., Donegal

A HOLD A HAND mirror in the grate and use it to view the skyward passage.

B. O. and Bad Breath

Q CAN YOU suggest a way of tactfully telling a work
colleague that he has very bad breath?

P.W., South Norwood

A I FIND IT helpful to use acting skills to tip off a
sufferer from 'death breath' without hurting his or
her feelings. Greet him, or her, as normally before springing back in surprise and horror, your face a mask of
affectionate revulsion.

'Good Lord!' you cry. 'What on earth have you been
eating? I've never smelt such a strong smell of garlic in
my life.' Often the offender will reply, 'I haven't eaten
any garlic,' in bemusement. If so, you can say, dramatically, 'You must have something trapped in your teeth,
then, because your breath is normally absolutely
alpine-fresh.'

Buoyed up by the idea that this is the *first time* they
have suffered from death breath, such people are often
willing to discuss the problem with their dentist. Cor-
poreal hygiene problems can be dealt with in a similar
manner. Springing back in amazement, you can say to
the offender, 'Good grief, what have you got in your
pockets? There's the most dreadful smell of rotten food
– you must have sat up against something somewhere
because you never normally smell badly at all.' Use the
optional codicil, 'but then I've just had my sinuses
cleared . . .', if you get no favourable response.

14

Boosting Sales of One's Own Book

Q I HAVE RECENTLY had the thrill of having a thin-
ly disguised autobiographical novel published.
Members of my immediate family are being wonderful
and ordering copies in bulk – but when they ring up
bookshops and give the same name as my own, it gives
booksellers the impression that my book is not of interest
to anyone outside my family. What can I do? I am nearly
distraught.

A.B., w8

A THANK YOUR relations for their kind interest and
loyalty but request that, when asked for their name
by booksellers taking these telephonic orders, they should
say in a throwaway tone 'John Mortimer' or 'Danielle
Steele'. These are magic names in the trade and will
cause a lot of backstage chitchat in the shop. 'John Mortimer's just rung up and ordered four copies of A.B.'s
book!' – and will spur the booksellers to take in large
stocks. When the time comes to collect their books your
relations need only masquerade as messengers – 'I've
come to collect the books for John Mortimer' – before
paying for their purchases in cash.

Buying a Present for a
Spoilt Godchild

Q I AM AT MY wits' end trying to think of a birthday present for a godson of four who, much to my disapproval, already has everything under the sun. His parents are inculcating him with consumerism. Can you suggest something I might get which, without being too schoolmarmy about it, could convey my disapproval for the excesses of his toy cupboard?

F.F., Spennithorne, Yorks.

A ONE UNUSUAL present – which is not available in toy shops – is a device called a nightingale. This imitative instrument, as used in the Toy Symphony of Haydn, can still be purchased at specialist music shops such as Boosey and Hawkes. On blowing it will produce a pleasing if slightly shrill warbling note, suggestive of the nightingale's song. Eventually, of course, its sound will act as a type of Chinese torture to those within regular earshot. By effecting this punishment on your godson's parents, you will be able to gain a discreet pleasure. If challenged you will have the additional satisfaction of being able to say, 'But it was the only toy he hadn't already got.'

By-passing Aides

Q CAN YOU recommend a method of by-passing secre-
taries and aides when telephoning so as to get
straight through to the man at the top? I am tired of
being fobbed off by underlings who ask if they can help
me as the man I want to speak to is 'rather tied up at
the moment'. I have an idea for a television series but I
cannot get through to Alan Yentob, Controller of BBC 2,
to discuss it.

David M., Shepherd's Bush

A YOU SHOULD ring up Mr Yentob's office and say,
'Hello. Could I have a very quick word with Alan?'
When the secretary enquires, 'Who's speaking please?'
you should half-sing 'David Yentobbbbb . . .' No aide is
likely to ask, 'Can I ask what it's in connection with?'
In such circumstances you are likely to be put straight
through. Yentob himself will take the call as he will be
intrigued to hear from a relation he has never met before.
Once you are 'through', Yentob will presume his aide
misheard your name or even that you gave his name by
mistake. In any case he will hardly hang up before you
have had a chance to give your spiel.

'Can I Pick Your Brains?'

Q HOW CAN ONE prevent people from ringing up and asking, 'Can I pick your brains?' I am a specialist bookseller. I have read an enormous number of biographies and letters and people know that I have a highly retentive memory. I don't often mind, but occasionally I feel rather resentful when people – especially young journalists and writers whom I have never even met – ring me up for information. Some of them are so arrogant they seem almost to expect me to virtually write the stuff for them just for the pleasure of hearing them say, 'Thanks, that's great,' as they put the telephone down. How can I say, 'No, do your own research' without seeming crabbed?

Name withheld, WI

A WHY NOT START banging your fist on your desk or table when such people ring you up? Then you can interrupt your callers as they begin to warm to their spiels by saying, 'I'm sorry – do you mind if I say I don't feel very inspired at the moment? We've got builders in and I really won't be able to think at all until they've left.'

Christmas Boxes for Dustmen

Q YOUR KIND advice please! It used to be a simple matter to give our dustmen a Christmas box. The refuse lorry always arrived round about the same time every Monday, a four-man team collecting and loading mostly in sight of each other. On hearing the lorry, which amusingly used to make much more noise just before Christmas, I would go out and give the money to the driver, asking him to divide it equally among the team. Thus most or all of them would witness this. At the beginning of this year, however, our local authority placed this service in the hands of a private firm, and the programme is different. One man now arrives in advance and places the black refuse bags from our dust-bins in our drive. The refuse lorry then collects them at widely unpredictable times – sometimes when we are not in. How can I ensure that my Christmas box to these dustmen will reach its rightful recipients this year?

E.W.H., Holly Bank, Ormskirk, Lancs

A A NUMBER of readers have written with similar queries, many of them concerned that the one dust-man who calls in advance, and whom one might see close to the house, should not siphon off the entire Christmas box for himself. My advice is that one of your refuse sacks should have Sellotaped to it a large sheet of white paper on which is printed in bold letters: 'REFUSE VAN DRIVER – PLEASE CALL AT THE HOUSE TO RECEIVE CHRISTMAS BOX.' If you are likely to be out when the driver might call, leave a similar notice on your front door which reads: 'REFUSE VAN DRIVER – PLEASE

CALL AT IVY BANK [or another adjacent property belonging to a co-operative neighbour] TO COLLECT CHRISTMAS BOX.' Readers should note that the dustmen's anticipation of Christmas boxes means that this is the best week of the year for getting rid of old fridges, garden refuse and other bulky items which dustmen normally refuse to take.

Christmas Presents for Mean People

Q CAN YOU please recommend a suitable Christmas present to be given to a very mean person? My husband's father has become almost pathological about saving money (despite having plenty of it). We are spending Christmas with him again this year and, as usual, it will be freezing cold, there will not be enough to eat or drink and there will not even be a television (he is too mean to buy a licence). We still give each other Christmas presents. Last year, however, I was rankled to realise that he saw even this as a means of saving money. To clarify: my husband, his brothers and I gave my father-in-law presents of cases of wine, jumpers, books etc. Meanwhile, each of us received in return a copy of one of those glossy books about Krishna given out in Oxford Street by Hari Krishna converts who ask you to pay 'what you can afford' for them. I would like to get my own back this year. What do you suggest?

A.F., St Peter's Square, Chiswick

21

A BUY HIM some television licence stamps. These are sold in £1 units and you should buy a frustrating amount such as £35 worth. As £35 is too much for a black and white licence and too little for a colour licence, your father-in-law will be doubly tormented. The stamps cannot be redeemed for cash and, no doubt, he will be too mean to make up the difference.

Church: The Etiquette of Interrupting Mass

Q I WAS IN MY local Catholic church on Sunday when a white-haired woman fainted or had a stroke in the bench in front of me. Luckily an Irishwoman and an aristocratic-looking Frenchman dealt with her. (The two Filipinos beside the woman did nothing and I am hopeless with sick people.) However, the Frenchman then turned to me and asked me to get a priest to fetch a doctor. My first instinct was to rush up to the side of the altar and interrupt the Mass but when I got there there were only two nine-year-old choirboys who did not understand my excited gesticulations. I became embarrassed about making a fool of myself in front of Antonia Fraser who was among the parishioners (as I know one of her sisters) so I walked back wondering what to do. Suddenly I remembered that a very disturbed man of my acquaintance was also among the congregation and in fact I had seen him handing out pamphlets at the back and going in a secret side door earlier to help with Parish matters. I rushed down the aisle, tapped this man

on the shoulder and whispered that a woman was dying near my pew. He acted promptly and went to the Porter's Lodge to call an ambulance. My question is: what is the correct procedure if this happens again? If I had not known this disturbed man (who, by the way, is a convert) would I have had to yell out and interrupt the Mass by shouting loudly for a doctor? My cousin, who like me is from a very old Catholic family – which, unlike that of the Duke of Norfolk's, never gave up its faith – says that priests are used to mad bag ladies shouting in Catholic churches and he would have taken no notice. When I asked Antonia Fraser, who by complete chance drew up outside my own front door after the Mass, what I should have done, she smiled charmingly but did not answer the question. My aunt, who is also from 'a very old Catholic family' but has gone ecumenical, says it wouldn't have mattered if the woman did die in church. What better place is there for her to die?

Troubled Catholic, Campden Hill Square

A IN THE CIRCUMSTANCES it would have been quite in order for you to approach the celebrant and interrupt him firmly and calmly. For future reference, however, you should acquaint yourself with the telephone facilities adjacent to the church so that you can move swiftly on your own initiative should something similar occur again.

Citroën Cars

Q PLEASE ADVISE me on the best way to bid farewell to visitors who have arrived in Citroën cars. Normally I like to escort guests out of the house, uttering the appropriate valedictory platitudes as I see them into their cars, and then wave them a final farewell on their disappearing down the drive. However, Citroën owners must wait for what seems an eternity while an inflation-.ary device slowly raises their car off the ground. During this period I am torn between abandoning them to their devices and going back inside – which seems abrupt – and extending my farewells with a stream of inanities. This dilemma has reduced me to a state of nervous exhaustion. Help please, urgently.

R.W., Nairobi, Kenya

A IN FACT YOUR friends are at fault here. It is up to them to insist that you go back into the house rather than hang around while they wait to be inflated. In order to punish them for their negligence in failing to do this, why not buy a pair of second-hand luggage weighing scales of the type used in railway stations and airports and have them installed outside your front door? The hydraulic suspension on these machines will, with a small adjustment by a trained mechanic, enable you to rise and fall in a mimicking process as you stand on the machine prior to your guest's departure.

Cleaning Up Before the Daily Lady Comes

Q I HAVE JUST engaged a daily lady. Can you give me any general advice on how much cleaning I need to do before she arrives? I am told by friends that the conditions in my flat are fairly squalid and I feel rather uncomfortable about asking someone else to clear it up for me.

A.B., w8

A HOUSEHOLDERS often make the mistake of cleaning up for the daily. Paradoxically dailies find this demoralising as they are thereby stripped of the satisfaction they could derive from making a visible impact on the chaos. Great pleasure is to be had from performing a simple physical task which brings order and, thereby, a degree of happiness, to another person. Therefore you should feel free to leave as much mess as you like for your daily to deal with.

Collection Boxes at the Door

Q WHAT IS THE best way to get rid of people who ring your doorbell and then stand there with a collection box for some charity or other? It's not that I am mean but I know plenty of people in my own immediate circle who need a pound just as much as someone I have never met in another country.

A.Q., w8

A IN LONDON it is perfectly easy to send the collector away empty-handed by saying. 'Sorry, there's no one in at the minute. I'm just cleaning up here.'

Conversational Irritants

Q I HAVE a friend whose husband, though amiable, is unremarkable save for the fact that he was educated in France. Possibly because of this, he takes care to introduce French words and phrases into any conversation and to pronounce them with their full complement of accents, garglings, etc. How can I explain, tactfully, that most people, nowadays, speak French just as well as he does and that to pronounce 'Marseilles' in the French manner when speaking to another English person is absurdly ostentatious?

C.A., London NW5

A ONE CANNOT reasonably expect a man who has gargled a word since childhood to pronounce it in the English manner. What one can expect, however, is for him to limit the number of French words, place-names and expressions he uses in conversation (though the poor chap is probably just trying to make himself seem more interesting). Perhaps you should deal with him by repeatedly interrupting his bursts of gargulosity to request clarification of what he has just said. Wear a pleasant but genuinely enquiring expression on your face as you do so. Take in his explanations and then repeat them aloud in dogged fashion as though trying to memorise them: '*au grand sérieux* – in all seriousness – *au grand sérieux, au grand sérieux*. That's a good one!!' etc. Soon he will learn to think twice before Frenchifying his conversation in your company.

Correct Number of Answerphone Messages

Q I AM A a 35-year-old bachelor living in London. I have just been away for a week's impromptu holiday. What is the correct number of messages to find on my answerphone on my return?

D.M., SW5

A YOU CAN have any number of business calls but a maximum of three personal calls for each day that you were away. Any more would indicate a lack of discrimination on your part or that you had acquired a reputation for social promiscuity.

Curing 'Roving Trotters'

Q HOW DOES one best cure the condition of 'roving trotters'? I enjoy cooking and having people to supper but find my hackles rising when certain friends come into the kitchen – supposedly to offer help or to chat to me. What they really want to do is start plucking handfuls of food out of whatever bowls and saucepans they can find, saying 'Mmm' as they uninhibitedly gobble down key nuggets of the dishes I am about to offer. How can I stop them without betraying my own greed?

H.M.M., Clanricarde Gardens, W2

A WHY NOT take up their offer of help as soon as they come through the kitchen door? Ask them to wash up, to chop an onion into tiny pieces or to hold a heavy tray while you load it for them – slowly and absent-mindedly. Thus manually disabled they will be in no position to give their trotters freedom to rove among the dishes you are displaying.

Dailies and Edible Panties

Q A GIRLFRIEND of mine gave my husband and me a so-called joke present of some edible panties for Christmas. My problem is that, having left these horribly packaged 'peach-flavoured' atrocities on my dressing table all over Christmas, my daily has now seen them. I returned from the New Year in Scotland and realised this. How can I throw them away without my daily thinking that we have 'used' the panties? The package comes with complete instructions on the outside about *how* to use them.

S.C., Wilts

A IF YOU DON'T own a dog, borrow one for a morning. Simply give the still wrapped package to the dog, having first played tug-of-war with him. Then release the dog into the room where your daily is cleaning and he can destroy the panties in front of her himself.

29

Despatching Motorcycle Messengers for Good

Q IMMEDIATELY outside my office is a small public park with benches upon which a collection of scruffy motorcycle messengers have recently started to appear while they wait for their next job to come over on their blaring radios. Can you suggest any method of encouraging them to move to a different part of the City? I have rejected danegeld as a solution.

J.B., EC2

A ASK A CO-OPERATIVE secretary to pop down to the park and tip off the messengers that the DSS has set up an investigative unit in your building, and that notes are being taken of their number plates and comings and goings. As an opinion-forming percentage of the messengers will be claiming dole money at the same time as executing their duties in the saddle, it should be only a matter of 24 hours or so before the last motorcyclist has got the message, and the annoyance you mention is at an end.

Dinner Following a Book Launch

Q THE PUBLISHERS of my book are very kindly giving a party for me next month and are about to send out invitations. I am looking forward to it, but wonder what one does about the social problem of which of one's friends one chooses to have dinner with afterwards? There are six or eight people I would prefer to go out with, but what should I say to the other friends, even to the marketing men – some of whom are bound to ask what I am doing or even if they can come too? The numbers could easily get out of hand and there could be clashes of temperament.

M.A., NW1

A THE MOST commonly used solution to this problem is that a close friend of the author holds a dinner for him or her in a private house following the launch party. This serves the twin purpose of giving the author an excuse to leave his own launch before it undergoes its final deglamorisation and of being able to say to second division friends, 'Oh I'd love to do something but so-and-so is holding a dinner for me.' Some authors even secretly give their own dinners. Explaining their predicament to a close friend with a conveniently located house, they slip him or her the 'readies' so that the friend can extend the invitations to the favoured few by proxy and can cater and serve on the night.

Disadvantage of Being an
Intelligence Agent

Q I WORK IN London for an American-owned private
intelligence agency. I have been personally involved in uncovering some of the most highly publicised
financial corruption scandals of the last two years. My
problem is that, though my work is far more interesting
than that of any of my contemporaries, I am – for obvious
reasons – unable to discuss it. I feel this puts me at a
disadvantage at dinner parties when girls, who know my
line of work but not precisely what I am working on, try
to coax me to tell them. How can I gracefully decline
and put an end to their insistent pleading, 'Go on, just
tell me a little bit about it,' yet still sustain their interest
in me?

Name withheld, London w1

A THERE IS ONE suave way in which you could
silence your questioners, yet stimulate their sus-
picions that you are a more interesting person than you
are allowed to reveal. Just give the cryptic response, 'It's
so top secret that if I tell you, I'll have to kill you.'

Disagreements over Dinner

Q LAST WEEK, at a small dinner party, I was introduced to someone who I wrongly believed to be a
friend of a friend of mine. I immediately said, 'I believe
you are a great admirer of X. So am I.' I was thrown
by her reply, 'I am certainly not an admirer of his! He
is an appalling man', and the subsequent list of crimes
of which she went on to accuse him. I quickly changed
the subject so as not to spoil the dinner party for everyone else by arguing in defence of my friend. But what
should I have done?

J.B., Chippenham

A ONE SOPHISTICATED way of agreeing to differ
over the merits of this mutual acquaintance would
have been to say languidly, 'How interesting. You're in
the anti-camp. People are always divided about him.' In
this way, you could have paid friendly respect to your
fellow guest's own judgment while simultaneously dis-
allowing the accuracy of her aspersions.

Discouraging a House-guest

Q SINCE I divorced two years ago, I have been living in a small, though well-appointed flat in central London. Originally I was pleased when, a few months ago, a former girlfriend who lives in the country started staying with me whenever she had to spend a night in London. I am now beginning to find it rather tiresome as she is quite bossy and rather takes over the place. There has been no resumption of intimacies between us as she is still happily married but she is beginning to treat me as a sort of supernumerary husband – even nagging me. I have told her that I feel she ought to stay less regularly as I enjoy being alone, but she waves this aside saying it is good for me to have a woman around as it will prevent me from becoming too crusty and eccentric. I am 43. How can I get rid of her?

Name withheld, w8

A NEXT TIME this former girlfriend telephones to advise you of an impending visit you can reveal that you find it too disturbing having her around, because the physical attraction towards her that you felt in the past has been re-aroused by the propinquity. Explain that you cannot guarantee that you will be able to resist a physical assault if she sleeps in close proximity to you again.

Discouraging Taxi Drivers from Chatting to One

Q WHAT IS THE best way to discourage a taxi driver from chatting, without appearing to snub him? I enjoy a chat when I am in the mood. Equally there are times when I prefer to concentrate on my papers or on my private thoughts. It is, of course, worse when travelling in a mini-cab without the glass partition.

I.L., W8

A IT IS ALWAYS best to enter the cab with a look of radiant friendship on your face. If the driver attempts to strike up a conversation in which you do not wish to participate, you can lean forward with a frustrated expression and say, 'I'm so sorry. I've had to take my hearing aid out because it was giving me a lot of interference.'

Dodgy Garages

Q HOW DOES one go about finding a garage where one will not be duped when one does not understand the first thing about cars and they can 'see one coming'?

A.A., Somerset

A DO JOIN THE RAC and take advantage of their free technical advice service. Staff at the centre will tell telephone callers exactly how much replacement parts cost – both new and reconditioned – and how many hours they will take to fit. Armed with this knowledge, you can expose your friendly local garage in its fraudulence.

Dog Messes

Q I LIVE IN Elm Park Road, Fulham, and ours is one of the very few houses in the neighbourhood to have a front garden. This means that we are plagued by inconsiderate neighbours who take their dogs for a walk at night, under cover of darkness, with the deliberate intention that the dogs should come into our garden to 'spend a penny'. I know this because I have even seen one person letting his dog off the lead outside our house. What can we do to prevent this?

Name withheld, sw3

A I AM FAMILIAR with the houses in question and suggest that you deal with the nuisance once and for all by having a cattle grid installed. This will be perfectly acceptable to the officials at the Royal Borough of Kensington and Chelsea providing that you are the owner of this access area. T. H. White of London Road, Marlborough, is a firm which would make up a 'dog grid' and be willing to arrange installation.

Dogs Barking Next Door

Q MINE IS THE usual barking-dog-next-door problem. Semi-detached Fulham house, marching with a charming and friendly woman, who goes out to work all day, and an inbuilt son, who works in and out of the house but sometimes disappears altogether. Whenever the dog is left alone he barks – not just sporadically, but continuously, relentlessly, inexorably, every note of which can be heard by me. My neighbour knows he does this, apologises for it, looks helpless when we meet, but clearly awaits divine guidance, doing nothing like thinking what can be done. Of course she has never suffered because the barking ceases the instant her car is heard or her footfall sensed. What can I do?

S.A., Haldane Road, sw6

A 'DEAR MARY' has received an enormous mailbag on the subject of neighbour abuse by dog – only one example of which is printed above. I suggest a drastic solution. S.A. should write herself a poison-pen letter purporting to come from a local cell of the Animal Liberation Front. The letter could perhaps be daubed in dried blood or have feathers glued onto it to give authenticity. It should be scrawled in a maniacal hand. The author should clearly have misunderstood the ownership of the barking dogs and be consequently levelling threats against S.A. She can approach the neighbours, poison-pen letter in hand, and suggest that, as the 'Animal Liberation Front are well known nutters', they deal with the problem at their earliest convenience to avoid violence.

Dorsal Harassment

Q I SOMETIMES find myself in the same position as the Queen: strange, common men put their arms around my waist or upper torso when ushering me or introducing me. She managed to show her displeasure (not that it did any good). How should I? Preferably without giving offence.

C.H., w2

A TRY CRYING out 'Sorry!' and jumping forward when you feel the first signs of dorsal harassment. Then turn and say, 'Oh sorry, it's you. I thought it was someone trying to push past me.' Then laugh pleasantly.

Dorsal harassment

Driving a 'Flashy' Car through a Deprived Area

Q I REGULARLY drive down to London from my farm
in Suffolk, hitting the East End round about pub
closing time. As I have a new BMW, I am beginning to
feel increasingly threatened by drunken youths at traffic
lights. Is there any foolproof way of deflecting the mob's
attention from my car?

T.B., Clare, Suffolk

A YOU MIGHT try the disguise of wearing dark reflective glasses which could help you to pass as an East End 'hood' or even as a local lad made good, such as David Essex. Another way of camouflaging yourself, or at least conferring solidarity, would be for you to chew violently on chewing gum with your mouth open when your car pauses at traffic lights.

Ducking Unwelcome Kisses

Q OVER THE festive season, I noticed that women were being kissed, willy-nilly, by a number of elderly men, i.e. relations, old family friends, whom they would normally keep at arm's length, as it were. The problem is not sexual harassment but halitosis: these men are increasingly proud of the fact that they have kept many of their own teeth, whereas in former times the offending molars would have been replaced by dentures. How can one avoid this situation?

F.M.B., Isleworth, Middlesex

A THE BEST way to avoid unwelcome oral assaults is to be prepared. As soon as you see a likely offender moving towards you, throw yourself clumsily against him. This will enable you 'accidentally' to kiss a part of his body – such as the side of his neck – which is out of fumes' reach and should preclude the need for any further intimacy.

Eating Noisily

Q MY SON-IN-LAW, otherwise a dear fellow, makes the most awful 'slushing' noise when he eats. This habit, particularly at the breakfast table, I find most difficult to bear. Apart from the use of ear-plugs with their obvious disadvantage, can you think of any solution for me?

B.B., Cornwall

A THIS IS A widespread problem and notoriously difficult to deal with. The only solution is to confide in close family friends and request their help. Set up a luncheon or dinner party with your son-in-law and these friends – ideally a married couple – present. The male member of the couple should make a loud slushing noise of his own as he eats. His wife can then intervene: 'I'm sorry, darling – you're doing it!' 'What? Good Lord, darling, no one minds a man enjoying his food. Look, X [your son-in-law] is far worse than I am – listen to that!' he can cry bluffly, as he makes the table listen to the sound effects coming from your son-in-law. He can then take up his fork again and eat even more noisily. 'No one minds except you, darling.' He can tell his wife before addressing each person at the table in turn to ask if they mind his making 'this slushing noise'? When it is your turn you can reply, 'Actually I do mind, since you ask. I mind very much. But I was brought up never to criticise another person's table manners . . .'

Ecoboring

Q MY WIFE has become an ecobore. Frankly we have plenty of money and she has very little else to think about other than her charity work for Green organisations. The trouble is that she has turned a virtue into a fault by becoming a sort of zealot. She now bores everyone, including all my family and friends, with streams of statistics and facts. She seems incapable of talking about anything else. How can I steer her back onto the general topics which we all used to prefer?

Name and address withheld

A YOU MIGHT suggest to your wife that she join the Islington-based Environmental Investigation Agency. This admirable company is the MI5/FBI of the Green world and looks into subjects such as government corruption in the ivory trade, etc. Were your wife to become involved in undercover intelligence work, even in a very minor capacity, there is no doubt that she would be advised by her superiors to publicly underplay her environmental commitments. She could then return guiltlessly to her former favourite topics of conversation.

Election Canvassers

Q WHAT IS the correct way of dispatching election canvassers who call at your house and whose party you do not support? I remember from the last election experiencing protracted embarrassment and boredom while enduring the 'spiels' of such people, but, short of shutting the door in their faces, what can you do?

F.W.W., Newbury

A DO REMEMBER that there are many lonely Britons who actually look forward to the visits of election canvassers and welcome them into their homes with eagerness. You should therefore feel no qualms about smiling brightly at your nuisance callers before saying, ambiguously, 'No need for you to waste any time here,' and directing them towards a neighbour who, you can confide, is very lonely.

Embarrassing Photograph

Q I AM A godson of a member of the Royal Family. I recently paid a visit to my family home and found to my dismay that my mother, who is a terrific snob, had unearthed a photograph of me with my godmother, and has displayed it on our piano in a prominent position. I was 17 at the time the photograph was taken. It is a full-length photograph. Like many boys, I was in a certain state of perpetual excitement when aged 17. It was no different on the day I was photographed and this is unfortunately all too obvious. How can I get rid of this embarrassing photograph? I cannot bring the subject up with my mother, who is very naïve.

Name and address withheld

A WHY NOT pose, in similar trousers, for another photograph? This should be taken by a co-operative friend. Having ensured that the perspective is correct, you may ask your photographic processor to enlarge the print to the correct sizing. Keeping a steady hand, you should cut out the new pelvis and trouser area and glue this neatly down on top of the original offending one. Using a camera suitable for close-up work, you can then re-photograph the whole, thus providing a negative which can be touched up in a darkroom so that none of the joins will be evident. The original can then be destroyed and the new acceptable photograph returned to its frame.

Encouraging Friendship
with Neighbours

Q I VERY MUCH enjoyed reading the excellent
memoirs of Quentin Crewe which were well
reviewed in your pages. A number of friends had already
suggested that they might be of interest to me as I too
am similarly disabled and – their words, not mine – 'have
an engaging personality'. My problem is that I have just
moved into a village where I know no one and my engaging personality may not be immediately apparent to
those neighbours, some more attractive than others, in
my terrace whom I see glancing at me from their
windows. How can I make friends with them? I am not
trapped in the cottage as I have an adapted car which
enables me to do the shopping.

O.W., Northants

A WHY NOT leave your car's headlights on when next
you park it outside your house? It won't be long
before someone comes round to tell you. Then you can
lure them into conversation, exercising the appropriate
amount of charm according to the desirability of the
neighbour as friend.

Etiquette of Gong-ringing

Q WHAT IS the correct way to ring a gong? I have just inherited one and would rather like to put it to use, but it has been so long since I stayed in a house where such an instrument was used to summon guests to dress or to dinner that I have forgotten the rhythm with which the blows should be struck, though I seem to remember that three is the correct *number* of blows.

S.B., Essex

A THREE GONG blows are no longer suitable as they bring the unconscious association with the tension which is introduced nightly around Britain by the opening moments of the *News at Ten* television programme. Far better to strike one single resounding blow, such as one sees at the start of the J. Arthur Rank advertising sequences in a cinema. Occasionally you might even perform this in a loin-cloth to amuse your guests.

Etiquette of Waving

Q WHAT IS the correct etiquette on waving? One thing that completely ruins country weekends for me is the business of waving goodbye to one's hosts as we drive away. Having already gone through the slightly embarrassing ritual of multiple kissings and declarations of enjoyment, I am never sure at what point I should stop waving or indeed at what point my hosts should stop waving, particularly if the car can be seen a long way from the house.

A.B., w8

A IT IS BEST to begin with a show of enthusiastic waving, then to abruptly simulate some difficulty from within the car – coat stuck in a door, contents of bag spilled out or similar. You can then simulate scrabbling on the floor of the car until you are almost out of sight of your hosts before turning round for one final gesture of enthusiasm.

Excessive Thank-you Letters

Q FOLLOWING our barbecue my wife and I received thank-you notes from almost every one of our guests. The consequence is that if we are invited back by any of our friends we will feel morally bound to send similarly effusive notes, a custom I have always resisted on the grounds that there is as much pleasure in throwing a party as in attending one. Has one of the Victorian books on etiquette been reprinted? Should we reciprocate by writing to thank them for their appreciative notes? What can we do to prevent the revival of this anachronistic courtesy?

C.G., Dippenhall, Surrey

A THE WRITING of thank-you notes has reached almost epidemic proportions in recent years and has arisen partially as a symptom of the so-called Brideshead Boom. Just as double-kissing is now practised by people such as photocopy machine mechanics, so thank-you notes have proliferated out of all proportion to the actual gratitude felt by the composers of the note. Sincere thank-you notes are undoubtedly received with happiness by those who have made an enormous effort, or who perhaps have unbusy schedules. For anyone with any sort of social life, however, adherence to the practice of writing such notes could mean their writing anything up to 21 a week. Such people's lives are regularly made wretched by the guilt and embarrassment they feel over not having written such letters. Many would agree with you that the guest often goes to as much trouble as the host when attending a dinner party. How many people actually want to go out on a cold winter's night, risking arrest for drunkenness, only to sit fully upright at a table being bright when they would rather be slumped on a sofa at home? One host of my acquaintance has dealt with the problem thus. When his guests are departing he simply announces, 'Will you forgive me if I don't write to thank you for coming – I never do. But it was so kind of you.' 'Good Lord,' his guests reply, 'There's no need for *you* to write. I was going to drop you a line. It's been such a lovely evening.' 'Nonsense,' he says firmly. 'The guest goes to far more trouble than the host. It's up to the host to be grateful.' Thus disconcerted his guests will go away, but he can be sure that, should he pay a return visit, there will now be no question of his being expected to write a thank-you note.

Extricating Oneself from a Conservation Group

Q WE LIVE IN London but have a house in the country. For some years now a couple of dear friends there have suggested we should join the local branch of a national conservation society. As nothing onerous beyond an annual subscription was involved and we thought the objectives of the society worthy, we finally joined. Our friends were delighted. To our horror, when we studied all the literature that flooded in, we found we did not agree with the policies or actions of the society. Worse, when we saw the list of members of the local branch, most of our local *bêtes noires* were among them. We are now being invited to attend meetings, rambles, *ad nauseam*. How do we resign from the society without hurting our friends?

Name and address withheld

A I PRESUME that, like many Englishmen, you are reticent about your personal finances and that no one beyond your immediate family has any idea of precisely how much you are 'worth' or how much you might or might not have lost at Lloyd's. You might, therefore, confide to your friends in the country that you have just been rescued from what you should describe non-specifically as 'big trouble' thanks to a windfall of a portfolio of shares which has come to you in the will of a distant relative. To your dismay, however, you find that the will has stipulated that you cannot move the shares into so-called conscience funds but must retain them in their existing companies. These are exclusively un-Green, being tobacco, defence, nuclear fuels and South Africa. Your friends are bound to understand that you must sadly tender your resignation from the society, as you cannot, in all conscience, continue to be a member in these new circumstances.

Failure to Identify the Foreign Secretary

Q I HAVE MARRIED into a politically active family despite having no interest in politics myself (I prefer racehorses). I regularly find myself in social juxtapositions with high-ranking cabinet ministers but I often have difficulty in recognising these people. To give an example, I was placed next to the Rt. Hon. Douglas Hurd at a recent fundraising dinner in an art gallery. I asked him what he did but failed to hear the word 'Foreign' in his job description so attempted to talk about makes of typewriter and typing speeds etc. What is a good all-purpose opening gambit by which I could encourage my interlocutor to reveal his or her status or position without betraying my own ignorance?

S.M., Fonthill

A WHY NOT use a variant of the Royal Family's opening gambit, which is, 'Have you come far?' by inquiring, 'What have you done today?'

Family Christmases

Q IS THERE any way that we can break the deadly and gruelling sequence of family Christmases this year? Each side of our family takes it in turns to play host and in theory it is a nice idea, but all too often deep resentments surface and the occasion turns sour. It is only August but the in-laws are pressing us for an answer.

K.C.W., Salop

A WHY NOT arrange to do charitable work on Christmas Day itself – such as helping out at a London shelter for the homeless? You can then set off, with a clear conscience and some like-minded friends, on Boxing Day, having arranged to stay until New Year at an agreeable sunspot in a remote corner of the globe. You need not spell out to your family the exact date of your departure.

Faxes

Q I AM THE editor of a well-known publication. On my desk I have a direct-line telephone whose number I have given out to only about seven people. Yet about three times, or more, per day, this line rings and I pick it up to hear the high-pitched beep of someone trying to send me a fax. How can I find out who this is and stop them?

D.L., WC1

A YOU WILL have to borrow a fax machine from another office in the building and plug it into your direct-line socket. Borrow one of the models which adapts itself to receiving either a fax or a telephone call and also flashes out the fax number of the person trying to contact you. In this way, you will be able to identify and punish the offender, who may well be a nuisance caller trying to annoy you.

Q YOUR PROBLEM from D.L., whose telephone line had been mistaken for a fax line, gave me food for thought. The other day I wanted to speak to my brother on the telephone, but couldn't face speaking to his wife first if she answered. One cannot just hang up. So I 'simply', as you would say, went to my office fax and dialled his home number. When my brother's wife answered I pressed the transmit button. The high-pitched beep, as fax-users will know, precludes conversation. There is therefore no way of identifying who is trying to get through. On the third try, my brother himself answered the phone saying, 'Oh good, it's you, some damn fool has been trying to send a fax through to us.' I offer you this solution to a problem that many of your readers are bound to have come up against in their own lives.

G.S., Stamford in the Vale

A THANK YOU for your considerate letter.

Five-minute Facelifts

Q MY PASSPORT has almost expired and I need to supply an up-to-date photograph of myself in order to renew it. I am 58 years old and my problem is that, though in real life I am remarkably well preserved by any standards, in posed photographs I look about 68. I believe this is because the face, when not animated, seems to sag downwards and forwards at my age. I cannot face carrying around a hideous picture of myself for ten years. What can I do? I just look like a loony if I try to 'animate' myself in the booth.

A.C., w8

A WHY NOT give yourself a temporary face-lift before entering the photo booth? This is only slightly painful and involves dragging the extra folds of sagging skin back and securing them with elastoplast behind your ears and at the top of your forehead. The elastoplast itself can then be masked by fluffing locks of hair over it. You will find the results to be remarkably effective.

Foul Language, Curbing
Children's

Q MY SMALL son, aged seven, has started at a very smart prep school and is picking up the most appalling language from the other boys. He is using terrible words that I have hardly even heard myself (I never watch television). How can I persuade him to stop it? He is obviously doing it out of bravado as he knows he will shock me and he does!

S.C., Hampshire

A TELL YOUR son that, actually, it is all right for him to use the new swear words he has learned. Add, 'As long as you don't use the really bad expressions such as "Shiver me timbers!" or "Dash!" which only a very bad boy would use.' You will find he will switch almost immediately to these more acceptable expressions.

Godchildren Not Writing
to Thank One

Q AS I AM A comparatively well-off bachelor, I have been made godfather to a number of friends' children. I am perfectly happy to be generous and usually quite good at remembering their birthdays, but I do find

it rather annoying when they don't write to thank or even acknowledge that they have had the cheque or present – or whatever I give them. How do other people ensure that their godchildren perform this simple act of politeness?

H.V., w8

A ONE POPULAR godfather who found himself in a similar position eventually tackled the problem by sending only a card on the birthdays of offending godchildren. The message inside would read: 'Happy Birthday. I enclose [for example] £10', yet he would not enclose any money at all. He found that the godchildren wrote back with alacrity to point out his oversight and, unable merely to make the bald request that he forward the promised cash, were forced to write a few lines of personal news. He continued to use it with satisfying results for many years. The understanding grew up, though neither godfather nor godchildren ever referred to it, that they must write their thank-you letters in advance.

Greeting Dilemmas

Q WHAT IS the correct thing to say to a friend who was *chef d'équipe* of a team at the Olympic Games when that team did badly? One cannot very well say 'Well done!', as it would be too obviously hypocritical. Nor can one pretend not to have been watching the whole thing on television, glued to every moment. I am going to meet the man in question at dinner next week. It will be the first time since before the games. What on earth shall I say?

Name and address withheld

A GREET YOUR friend with the usual physical gusto but instead of saying, 'How are you?' – shout 'What *ha*ppened?!!!!!!' Practise saying 'What *ha*ppened?' beforehand so that you get exactly the right inflection to imply that, whatever happened, it was certainly not his fault.

Guests with Mildewed Clothing

Q OUR FRIENDS from Queensland came to stay a couple of years ago and we soon noticed that their clothes, dresses and suits had a strong smell of mildew. I believe this is hard to avoid in warm climates. They are obviously not aware of the problem as their sense of smell has lost its sensitivity to this particular odour. We

look forward to another visit shortly and wonder:
1. How we can let them know they have a problem?
2. How we can get the smell out of their wardrobe when they have gone?

A WAIT UNTIL your guests have unpacked, then leave a large note on the kitchen table saying, 'MRS A —, WHAT DO YOU WANT ME TO DO ABOUT MIL-DEWED CLOTHES IN GUEST WARDROBE?' Ensure that your guests see the note – which you can pretend has been written by your daily help. If you have no daily help, you can always pretend you have one sporadically. Your wife can feign perplexity as she studies the note and says, 'Good Lord! I am sorry. I thought I had cleared out that wardrobe so you could have it all to yourselves.' Stalking into the bedroom with your friends in tow, you can fling the wardrobe door open, then say, 'Phew! This wardrobe stinks of mildew. I'm so sorry! But hang on a minute – it does seem to be coming from your clothes. How could that have happened? Perhaps they became damp on the journey over . . . ? etc., etc.' You can then open up a good-natured debate about mildewed clothing and conclude that the Australian nostril must lose its sensitivity to this particular odour, as you seem to remember now hearing about this mildew problem before from other people with Aussie friends.

Hair Hygiene

Q MY PARTNER and I have suffered the social in-
adequacies of a mutual friend for too long and we
feel we must seek your advice to counter this problem.
The person in question seldom washes his hair and, when
he actually does, seems to insist on using an inferior
shampoo and, to boot, no conditioner. (Hence the rather
unattractive split ends.) How do we convey to this person
that it's high time he washed his hair, and what's more,
cut it?

S. and M.J., Manchester

A ENLIST, AS an accomplice, a friendly, junior, local
hairdresser. Junior hairdressers are notoriously
badly paid, so he or she will no doubt be happy to co-
operate with you for a small fee. Give the hairdresser
your friend's address and arrange for him to receive a
letter along the following lines: 'Dear Sir, I'm sorry I do
not know your name but I have often seen you walking
past our salon and once or twice have noticed you go
into this house. I have taken the liberty of writing to you
and wonder if you would think it very cheeky of me to
request that I might be allowed to wash and cut your
hair at no charge to yourself. I want to specialise in
"transformation hairdressing" and the local paper has
agreed to do an article about me if I can find a suitable
client whose appearance would be dramatically im-
proved by a washing and cutting treatment. I feel that
you are a perfect subject for me to practise on as you
have such potential to be transformed by hairdressing
and would be grateful if you would consider this request

from a junior hairdresser and be in touch with me to arrange a time suitable for yourself. Yours sincerely . . . etc.' This should do the trick.

'Hand-me-downs'

Q MY DAUGHTER of four is exactly one year older than my god-daughter of three. As children grow out of clothes in so short a time, it makes sense for me to pass on my daughter's clothes to my god-daughter who is exactly the right size for them, season by season. My problem is that I also wish to claw back these loaned items – some of which are fairly high quality – as I have another daughter of one. How can I make an accurate inventory of what I have loaned?

F.B., Essex

A WHY NOT pin the tiny garments to a washing line once you have assembled a batch, for recycling – and then photograph them. In this way you will serve the twin purposes of practicality and social history. The photograph will be an invaluable aid to the recovery process and it will also provide a record which, in as little as ten years' time, will give a fascinating glimpse of the typical wardrobe of a three-year-old girl of today.

Hideous Heirlooms

Q MY 70-YEAR-OLD parents inherited a sizeable sum
of money from a great aunt two years ago. Unfortunately they have appalling taste and, instead of spending
the money on travelling, or taking advice and snapping
up some of the bargains currently available in the sale-
rooms, they have fallen into the terrible trap of buying
heritage offers from the Sunday supplements. Their walls
are lined with collections of commemorative thimbles
and miniature vintage cars, reproductions of the Mappa

Mundi and facsimiles of the Domesday book. They honestly believe that one day these things will be heirlooms and, still worse, that I, as their ultimate recipient, will treasure them. I know my parents better than to criticise them to their faces. What can I do to stop them?

R.K., Blandford

A YOU COULD communicate with a leading auction house, suggesting that its local representative in your parents' area should get in touch to view 'an extraordinary collection' and value it for insurance purposes. No doubt your parents will jump at the opportunity of discussing the sky-rocketing value of their investment and will agree to a meeting. There should be no need for you to take any further action.

Hideous Ornaments

Q OUR VALUED daily has begun to give us presents in the form of what she calls 'ornaments'. These *objets* include things like two-foot-high green Buddhas, which she has brought back from holidays with her family in the Far East, and giant glass animals in garish colours. We do not find these things attractive to behold, yet have had to place them on reasonably prominent display so as not to hurt our daily's feelings. How can we discourage her from buying us any more presents like these? More to the point, how can we get rid of the existing ones without upsetting her?

G.C., London WII

A PERHAPS you already have a house or cottage in the country in addition to your London premises? If not, why not invent the recent rental of such a property for weekend purposes? You can then enthuse to your daily that her ornaments look wonderful in this venue where they 'can be displayed to their best advantage'. Any further presents can be greeted with similar enthusiasms as 'they will look so lovely in the country'.

Holiday-let Hiccoughs

Q FOR TEN YEARS we have let our holiday home in France very cheaply, but only to family friends. This has worked very well, with some families returning every year. Breakages and phone calls have been reported and paid for. This year, however, we have discovered that someone has broken the on/off switch on the television and attempted to glue it back on. The switch is useless – the television will not work. Even more distressing than the expense and inconvenience incurred is the disappointment that one of our friends has been so dishonest. Can you suggest some means by which we could discover who did this, without offending the others who have used the house this summer?

F.C. and J.M.C., Kent

A YOU SHOULD ring round all the friends who stayed during the period in question. Ring them by rota of the date of their visit. Say to each one in turn, 'I'm just ringing to thank you for having left the money to pay for the repair of the television switch. We had no idea you had left the money under the set otherwise we would have rung to thank you sooner. We have only just come across it.' Innocent parties will reply, 'Oh, it was actually broken when we arrived!' Guilty parties will hesitate before replying, 'Actually we didn't leave any money.' The really criminally inclined will hesitate doubly before saying, 'I hope it was enough.' At which point you can say, 'Oh dear, I'm afraid it wasn't. We had to replace the whole set. Any chance you can get the rest out of your holiday insurance?'

How Can I Tell Whether or Not Someone Fancies Me?

Q HOW CAN I tell for certain whether or not someone fancies me? I have been 'going out' for a few weeks with a girl who does seem to enjoy my company, and though she comes round to my flat, where I could in theory make a pass at her, I have so far been too feeble to do so. I am fine once over the initial hurdle but the truth is that it's never been me that has made the first move. In the past, I have always let the girl make her feelings known. This one has not yet made any such demonstration and may, or may not, be waiting for me to do so. What should I do? I could not bring myself to just lunge and risk her drawing away in revulsion, having thought we were just friends.

P.W., SE17

A YOU SHOULD arrange to meet the girl in question in your flat for drinks before a night out. Adopt a stupefied demeanour and explain, as she arrives, that you are incredibly sorry – you have stupidly taken travel sickness pills instead of Panadol and are having difficulty focusing and concentrating. 'I'd better not mix them with alcohol, I suppose, but *you* have a drink. Let's stay here for half an hour or so and see if I sharpen up a bit.'

The key purchase you should make before this encounter is a Feverscan thermometer. This illuminated strip is held against one person's forehead by another and affords a desirable degree of physical intimacy. Having asked her to take your temperature you can then collapse on top of her rather than lunge. Should this be met with a physical stiffening on her part, you may simply allow her to restore you to your upright posture. Should you sense that it has been met with acceptance you may then fasten your lips on hers with confidence.

Ignoring 'Chatty' Passers-by

Q MY HUSBAND is a DIY fanatic. He is currently cobbling the area in the area in front of our house in a listed village. It is a painstaking job which he is tackling with admirable precision. Unfortunately, he is being driven almost mad by the number of visitors to our village who seem to think he is part of some sort of heritage re-enactment of traditional skills and who come up, chuckling, to chat to him. What is the most dismissive answer my husband can give when tourists say to him 'You've got a job on there!' or 'Are you winning?' He does not wish to be rude.

G.A.W., Astbury

A YOUR HUSBAND would do well to purchase a pair of protective ear-coverings as worn by users of power-drills. In order to give them validity, he need only allow an electric drill on a flex to dangle from your own household to grace the cobblestones. In this way he can simply ignore tourists without giving offence.

Inviting Oneself

Q IS IT ACCEPTABLE to telephone fairly good (though middle-aged) friends from a train which is about to pass through their part of the country, and ask if you can get off and come and stay the night with them?
E.H., Amwell Street, ec1

A YES, YOU may surprise them with such a request, provided you take the following precautions. Ring up and put the proposition to the friends. Then immediately, before they have a chance to be embarrassed or panicked into accepting, say, 'Hang on, I'm running out of units. I'll go and buy another phonecard and call you back in about ten minutes.' This will give the couple a chance to dither in their own home about whether or not middle age has made them too inflexible to enjoy surprises of this nature. It will also give them time to have made up an excuse by the time you ring back.

John Simpson's Problem

Q LAST JUNE, in the depths of the Brazilian jungle, the local shaman had prepared an unpleasant-smelling, hallucinogenic brew for his village, and a beaker of the stuff was ladled out and handed to me. I had heard that strange and nasty things happened to those who drank it; so I indicated that I would take just a single sip. As I put it to my mouth, I became aware that everyone was making signs to me that I should drink the entire cup: a very large one. Various things happened in the hours after that: a six-foot goldfish in a straw hat put its fin round my shoulder and asked me how I was, for instance. I didn't know how to answer him and I didn't know how to decline the full drink. How should I have replied to the shaman?

John Simpson, BBC, London W12

A I CONSIDER my solution to be something of a breakthrough. It will benefit intrepid newsmen and even teenagers being urged to swallow dangerous toxins by their peers. Purchase a 'Femidom', the new female prophylactic. This has a diameter of roughly three inches at its 'entrance' point. Pop the prophylactic into your mouth – having first removed the detachable plastic ring at its farthest end. Allow the balloon-shaped slack to sit comfortably on your tongue. 'Fit' the opening ring so that it sits between your teeth and lips. The device, which is opaque-coloured, is now invisible and can be left *in situ* to collect unwanted drinks, pills, even a limited amount of foodstuffs, which you can then expel discreetly once the focus of attention has moved from you.

Keeping Children Quiet

Q I WAS INTERESTED to read your recent suggestion of a nightingale musical instrument to give to a child who has everything. May I offer you a suggestion of my own? Bubble packaging – used for wrapping china and precious things which are to travel by post – can be bought in huge rolls – so big you have to fit them into the back of a Range Rover – from Ryman for £30. I always keep a roll and bring a 'length' tied with a pretty ribbon, when I am going to visit a house with a small child in it. The bursting process keeps them occupied for hours.

C.C., w8

A THANK YOU for your amusing suggestion.

Key Pimples

Q I HAVE A large staphyloccocal pimple in the centre of my forehead. I am due to attend an important wedding next weekend. How can I cover up this eyesore? All the masking agents I have attempted to use have resulted in caking – just making it look like a piece of millefeuille pastry with a spot in the centre, rather than just a plain spot.

C.G., Wilts

A WEAR A PLASTER over the pimple on the day of the wedding. Tell fellow guests that you were injured by a thorn when pruning roses. This will make your injury seem quite glamorous.

Kippers for Breakfast

Q ON AN IMPULSE that I now regret, I asked the hall porter at my London club if I could have kippers for breakfast. As a result he spoke to the housekeeper who brought them to my bedroom, as requested, at 7.30 in the morning. She commanded the chambermaid to lift the cover and what was revealed but two headless and tail-less, pallid poached kippers floating in a shallow sea of lukewarm water? The housekeeper then assured me that willy-nilly I should have kippers every time she found my name in the book as staying at the club overnight. This was a special privilege. They tasted like evil-flavoured wet cotton-wool, so how can I arrange to revert to bacon, eggs and a sausage, without offending the good woman?

J.R.E.S., Whitsbury

A YOU COULD perhaps say to the hall porter that he should ask the housekeeper to forget her promise to provide kippers indefinitely. Confide that a distant cousin has recently been lost at sea between Scarba and Jura in the Gulf of Corryvreckan and that you can no longer face the thought of fish, kippered or otherwise.

Lavatories and
Working Breakfasts

Q MY HUSBAND is shortly to attend his first ever
'working breakfast' at which he will be meeting
some American politicians. He has asked me to write to
you because he is concerned that he may have to leave
the table at a disadvantageous moment. Having been
trained from his early days in the nursery, and then all
through prep and public school, to go to the lavatory
directly after breakfast, he has an almost Pavlovian reac-
tion to his cornflakes. What is more, he is accustomed
to expending a fairly lengthy period of time there. Can
you suggest some way in which he can avoid the annoyance he will cause by keeping the Americans waiting
impatiently for his return to the table?

S.B., SWI

A IT WOULD be best for your husband to get up in
time to have a light breakfast in the privacy of his
own home before setting out for the working breakfast.
He should consume just enough to trigger the expulsion
process. This can then be effected in the normal manner,
enabling him merely to toy with his secondary breakfast
and – with all physical needs satisfied – to give his full
concentration to his American companions.

Lavatory Blockages

Q WHAT IS THE best way of dealing with the problem of lavatory blockage? My wife and I have four daughters, each of whom brings teenage girlfriends home for weekends. The receptacles which we have provided in each lavatory are ignored, and we do not wish to display ostentatious notices referring to sanitary appliances. Over the years, the increasing cost of drain clearance has soared to an intolerable level of £300 per annum and a remedy is sought.

Name withheld, Glos.

A WHY NOT take your cue from one of our leading stately-home owners, each of whose lavatories is equipped with a box of tissues positioned at the eye-level of the person using the lavatory? A stick-on label on each tissue box announces, 'Please do not throw tissues down loo but into bin provided or blockage will occur.' The owner in question finds that her guests are clearly surprised enough at the idea that tissues might block a loo to go on to consider the further implications. She has had no more problems since the strategically placed boxes were introduced.

Lazy Daily

Q I HAVE A problem with my daily. She started a
month ago and supposedly comes on Tuesdays and
Thursdays, but each time she seems to do less work than
the time before. The person who recommended her says:
'Please don't sack her. She's such a nice person, she is
having some problems at home.' However, last week I
would hardly have known she had been at all were it not
for the fact that she had taken the money. I am out at
work all day so I never see her. What can I do?

L.B., Aldridge Road Villas, WII

A JUST DON'T leave the money next week. When
your daily rings up and leaves a message asking
that she be paid, you can explain in astonishment that
you did not leave the money because you didn't realise
she had been.

Limiting a Party List

Q I WANT TO give a 40th birthday party for my husband but have been rather put off the idea by a friend whose own 40th birthday party was the cause of far more rancour than celebration. 'Never give a party, is my motto,' he says. 'You just make a whole new set of enemies amongst people you don't ask.' Our problem is that we can only invite 60 people, and there are certain people who aren't as old friends as others yet whom we would prefer to have. How can we get around this problem as everyone we know knows one another and will know the party is happening?

C.H., Worcs.

A THE KEY thing to do when giving small 40th birthday parties is to issue the invitations verbally. Printed invitations will be displayed on mantelpieces and cork-boards, where people who are not invited will see them and be upset. Ring around the friends you do want – giving them plenty of notice – and say, 'It's Charles's birthday on the such-and-such. Will you come to dinner?' Underplay the grandeur of the occasion (though say, 'I'm wearing my new dress because I thought it would be nice if we dressed up a bit') and let people be pleasantly surprised when they arrive to see hordes of others. Those invited will not have had time to whip up envy among people who are not and, because 'important' parties are inextricably linked to stiff white invitation cards for most people, the fact that these were never issued will be enough to diminish the party's importance in the minds of those who were not asked.

Loos, Etiquette of Flushing

Q I RECENTLY attended an international seminar at a most prestigious country house. I shared a bathroom with a colleague whose bedroom also adjoined it through a separate connecting door. During the night, I had an unanticipated call of nature. I faced a dilemma. Should I have pulled the chain – in which case I would almost certainly have woken up my doubtless worn-out colleague? Or should I have pursued a policy of masterly inactivity, in which case my doubtless sensitive neighbour, though fully refreshed, would have been faced with an aesthetically undesirable start to his day? I pursued the latter course, but remain uneasy. What do you suggest for next time?

A.M., Twickenham, Middlesex

A I SUGGEST you lay a 'bed' of lavatory paper over the offending matter so that it is at least invisible to your colleague first thing the next morning. I also advise leaving a handwritten notice, attached to the closed lavatory lid, stating 'Out of Order'. The inconvenience to your colleague, of finding another lavatory in a country house, would be minimal compared to what he otherwise might experience.

Losing the Heel of a Shoe

Q WHAT IS the drill when losing the heel of a shoe during a weekend, when no shoe menders or indeed shoe shops are available?

C.L., WII

A DRIVE TO the nearest motorway round-about where you will find a selection of odd shoes on the grassy verge. You will, more than likely, be able to find a shoe there to fit you in a similar style to the one which has been damaged.

Maiden Names

Q MY WIFE uses her maiden name for professional purposes, and is known by that name in her job as a publishing director. She is enraged, and regards it as little short of impertinence, if she is addressed on an envelope, at home or at work, as Mrs G—G—, which I assure her is correct usage. 'On the contrary,' she says, 'it is an archaism and its continued usage explains much of what is wrong with our society today.' She similarly thinks I'm antiquated in addressing letters to members of the male sex as, as it were, Joe Bloggs, Esq., rather than Mr Joe Bloggs or plain Joe Bloggs. How can I persuade her of the rightness of my point of view?

G.G., London NW5

A of course you are correct in adhering to these harmless traditions which are intended to be nothing more than gestures of all-purpose courtesy, dating from a time when it was considered desirable to be either a lady or a gentleman. Perhaps, however, you could make a compromise towards your wife's intractable position by taking your cue from certain male American feminists or 'hag fags' who allow themselves to be addressed by their wife's name as a gesture of solidarity, i.e. Mr Katharine Black. Were you to start receiving a percentage of mail addressed in this way, it might serve to placate your wife and make her hold a less severe view on the subject.

Making Guests 'Come Through' When Food is Ready

Q I am giving a number of dinner parties over Christmas and would like to ask your advice on a point of control. What can one do when people just carry on laughing, talking and drinking when you have told them that supper is ready and have asked them to come through to the dining room? It is particularly annoying if you are having soup or a soufflé, which I am planning to. Can you advise a foolproof way of getting my guests to come through when they are asked to?

M.P.C.M., Wilts

A that first flush of intoxication which characterises the moods of many guests at the beginning of a dinner party tends to render them unco-operative about 'coming through'. Often they are mid-anecdote with a new person and the alcohol has diminished their sense of responsibility when the call to table is given. You should have no trouble in getting them to come through, however, if you switch off the lights in your drawing room shortly after your announcement is made. The pitch darkness will bring your guests to their senses and you will find that they blunder swiftly out towards the light and the dining room.

Militant Ramblers

Q WE HAVE recently had a rights of way warden open a long-forgotten footpath which crosses our land very close to the house. This has infuriated my husband

who now patrols it obsessively, lecturing hapless ramblers on their rights, their dogs and the country code. Unfortunately the conspicuous signpost has attracted a new breed of militant rambler, who seems to relish these agrarian arguments and inflames my husband still further. I am finding his Basil Fawltyism emotionally exhausting. What should I do?

M.W., Wilts.

A MOST WALKERS are harmless types who stick to footpaths religiously. However, to distract your husband from the immediate annoyance of the new breed of militant rambler, why not suggest that he excavate, quite legally, several 'mantraps' in the field in question but at some distance from the path. These should be four or five feet deep and will soon fill up with water after which they may be covered with a camouflage of sticks and vegetation similar to those used in the book *Rogue Male* by Geoffrey Household. Your husband can then redirect his energies as the sight of approaching ramblers will begin to fill him with anticipation rather than rage.

Mispronunciation of Grosvenor

Q WHAT DO YOU do when someone you are talking to mispronounces a word? This happened to me recently when someone I was talking to pronounced the word Grosvenor Gros-ven-or. I did not like to correct her as she was the sort of person who might have felt 'put down', yet I myself wanted to say the word Grosvenor, indeed knew I was going to have to, sooner or later in the conversation which took place at a drinks party. As a result I said 'Gros-ven-or' too, but I am sure that since our conversation she will have found out the correct pronunciation and feel that I have been making fun of her. What should I have done?

A.N.W., w8

A YOU COULD have avoided 'putting down' your interlocutor by also mispronouncing the word yourself, but in a different wáy to hers. Then you could have said, as the conversation continued, 'You know, I don't think either of us has got this pronunciation right. Let's ask a third party for an opinion.' When you are both exposed as being incorrect your interlocutor will feel a sense of camaraderie rather than inferiority.

Mispronunciation of 'one'

Q EVERY TIME I listen to television or radio these days I hear people from all walks of life saying 'wan' instead of 'one'. I find this deeply annoying but perhaps I have missed some new development in vocal etiquette. Is it now correct to say 'wan'? I do hope not.

K.M., Oxford

A NO, IT IS not correct. What has happened is that when broadcasters who hail from the north of England have to modify their regional accents for reasons of nationwide clarity 'wan' is the last thing to go. Such people then speak 'BBC English' peppered with 'wans' and the habit has spread insidiously among the mentally passive. One – as in won – is still correct.

Missing Balls

Q FOR MANY years I have kept two balls (wooden, ping-pong size), for purely sentimental reasons, usually on my dressing-table but occasionally in other places to give them a change of scene. About a fortnight ago I could find them nowhere. How do I ask our 'daily', a not unattractive but very high-minded young lady, where she may have put them – bearing accusations of sexual harassment in mind?

B.S. (aet 71), SW1

A ARRANGE FOR A female friend to call at a time when your daily is likely to be present and ask you, within earshot, 'Where are those charming little wooden balls you used to display about the place?' You can then reply, 'You're right – where are they? I haven't seen them myself for a long time. Have you any idea, Janet?'

Mistaken for
The Rt. Hon. Douglas Hurd

Q MY HUSBAND bears a striking resemblance to the Rt. Hon. Douglas Hurd MP. He is frequently being mistaken for him in restaurants. What can we do to prevent further embarrassing incidents?

S.I., London W8

A MOST CHEMISTS sell a vegetable hair colourant called henna, which can be used without harsh or drying repercussions to turn the hair an unnatural and striking shade of red. The dye can be mixed in a disposable plastic bowl and your husband could apply it by standing with his head upside down in this bowl for only 20 minutes. This should help you to cut out any further difficulties of mistaken identity.

More Fancying

Q I ENJOYED reading your advice to the man who was unsure whether or not the girl he was taking out 'fancied' him. My problem is also a romantic one but I do not even know the name of the man for whom I have conceived a passion. We often sit in the same carriage while commuting into Oxford, and he appears to blush when I go past him. I feel it is possible that he likes the look of me as much as I do of him, but is too shy to do anything about it. How can I find out who he is and, from there, try to bump into him in a social context?

Y.M.G., Didcot

A IT SEEMS likely that you and your potential romantic partner live within a reasonably confined radius of one another. One way of ascertaining his identity would, therefore, be for you to offer your services to some likely local charity as a seller of raffle tickets. You could then quite routinely approach the young man in question, in line with all the other commuters in the carriage. Make sure you charge only a laughable sum – such as 10 or 20 pence – for each ticket and he will almost certainly be able to afford one. The purchase will enable him not only to strike up a conversation with you but also to give you his name and address. Armed with this knowledge, you may make further enquiries.

Names, Forgetting People's

Q LIKE COUNTLESS others, I have a terrible memory for names and consequently struggle for terms with which to address friendly but forgotten faces. While 'darling' and 'my dear' suffice surprisingly often for members of the opposite sex, 'squire' and 'sir' for other men are too horribly jocular, fit only for the saloon bar and the lesser sort of golf club. 'Mate' is obviously beyond the pale ('dear boy' fits the bill from time to time but overuse may lead to one being considered homosexual or a luvvie). That great bloodstock agent Frankie More O'Ferrall used to address all comers as 'friend'. Coming from him it seemed dignified and appropriate but I don't seem able quite to get away with it. Can you suggest some polite form of address to drop into the conversation until such time as the penny finally drops?

J.L., Dublin

A HOW ABOUT 'boss'? The flattery implied by this term can only be interpreted favourably no matter where, in terms of rank, you and your addressee stand in relation to each other.

More Forgotten Names

Q PLEASE SUGGEST a solution to a problem I personally experience at least once a week – this is of
running into someone who I know I know, but being
quite unable to remember their name or what they do.
Flattery and ego-nursing are integral parts of my job (I
work in publishing), so you can see how these failures
to identify people can be damaging, quite apart from
the fact that they are horrendously embarrassing. What
should I do? I am beginning to dread going out.

D.L., SW1

A WHY NOT carry permanently in your pocket or
wallet a petition in aid of some anodyne cause that
anyone would be willing to support? There should be
spaces for signature, name in block capitals, and work
address. You can then withdraw this from your pocket
the moment you spy a mystery figure advancing and say
fervently, 'How wonderful to see you. May I ask you to
sign my petition?' before you launch into any general
chat. Another method which can be used by people who
do not wear glasses is to stare blankly in the direction of
the person who has said hello and reply, 'You'll have to
tell me who it is. I haven't got my contact lenses in and
I can't see a thing.'

Nasal Hair

Q A CHAP IN the social clique to which I belong is a splendid fellow by anyone's estimation. However, he has the most prolific and unsightly growth of nasal hair. How does one broach the suggestion of its removal without causing embarrassment to all the parties concerned?

Name and address withheld

A WHY NOT suggest to your friend that he pose for a black and white silhouette portrait? In this way the artist can draw attention to the unsightly nasal hair you mentioned in a tactful manner and no repercussive embarrassment need attach to you personally.

Neighbours – a Fallen Frieze

Q SOME YEARS ago, a very decorative piece of exterior moulding fell down from the frieze around my neighbours' house (almost killing me). As the house was unoccupied I retrieved the moulding and over the years it has become an essential component of a rather pretty grotto in my garden. My problem is that I now have new neighbours who have done up their house and there is a conspicuous gap in the frieze where 'my' piece of moulding should belong. As I am now good friends with the newcomers, how can I avoid their noticing the contraband when they have drinks in my garden, which is planned any day now?

J.S., w8

A LEAD YOUR neighbours out into the garden – show them the grotto and moulding and reveal to them that you had a tug of conscience about giving it back to them. You can afford to be perfectly honest because, in fact, it would be cheaper and easier for a builder to take a cast from your moulding to produce a new one to fill in the frieze than for him to try and remount the original unsafe one.

Neighbours and Eyesores

Q I LIVE IN a glorified council house which I hope
the council-tax assessor will regard as terraced but
which estate agents would otherwise describe as 'link
detached'. My neighbour is an amiable man, coming
from a distant part of the United Kingdom; but he is
lethargically indolent. When he acquired a new car he
left the old derelict one on his driveway outside his garage and the new one is parked behind it towards the
road. In getting in and out of his car he takes great care
not to walk on my garden, but the postman and the
milkman and others do not. Having already asked about
the disposal of the old car, how can I cause it to disappear
without starting a feud?

L.E.H., Colchester

A ARRANGE for a secondhand-car dealer or scrap-
metal dealer to call around at a time when your
neighbour is not likely to be in. Ask for a valuation of
the car's worth as though you are the owner. You may
then proceed towards asking your neighbour if you can
buy the car for yourself. Offer him the figure you have
been quoted. If he accepts you may pay up and get your
dealer to come and take it away within a couple of days,
telling your neighbour that you had found the car unsuit-
able for your purposes after all.

News Addicts

Q MY PARENTS are hooked on the news. First the six o'clock news, then the nine o'clock news, and then the ten o'clock news – my father says he likes to 'see the different angles'. The panic-mongering music which precedes the news seems to bring on a sort of conditioned reflex. They drop everything and rush to the television. How can I deprogramme them?

A.S.K., Thorpe-le-Soken

A IT MIGHT be salutary for you to tape the music of *News at Ten* or one of the other frightening theme tunes, and play it at random intervals during the day. Your parents will rush, in Pavlovian manner, to the television set for as many times as it takes them to see the humorous nature of their addiction. Try playing the tape in the middle of the night when they are asleep.

Nicknames

Q I AM A racehorse trainer and my Christian name is James – or Jimmy, as many of my friends call me. However, following a recent run of successes on the race-course, journalists have been referring to me in print as Jamie, my least favourite diminutive. I do not wish

87

to appear ungrateful for the nice write-ups that followed these wins, so how can I tactfully put a stop to this Jamie business?

J.T., Newmarket

A contact the Newmarket correspondents of the *Racing Post* and *Sporting Life* and ask them to spread the word that you have a cousin of the same surname and whose Christian name is Jamie. Say that your cousin is shortly to take up a position in public life which may engender newspaper coverage. To avoid possible confusion, you therefore suggest that in future you be referred to in print as either James or Jimmy – 'the name by which I am known to most of my friends'.

Nigel Nicolson's Problem

Q in the national trust shop attached to my house they sell, among many others, copies of my own books. One of the shop-ladies asked me to sign a copy for her. I crossed out my name on the title-page and rewrote it underneath. 'Oh please put my name too,' she said. I should have known it, because she has been there several years. I thought it was Sally. To make sure, I asked, 'I forget – is it Sally with a "y" or an "ie"?' 'Who's Sally?' she said. What should I have replied?

N. Nicolson, Sissinghurst Castle, Kent

A YOU SHOULD have whispered, 'I'm sorry. It's just that you remind me so much of a girl I was in love with as a young man. Her name was Sally.' Then, suddenly coming to your senses, you could have said more formally, 'Of course I know what yours is but can you spell it for me?'

Noisy Neighbours

Q HOW CAN one prevent neighbours from making unacceptably loud noises during the process of intimacy? A rather show-offy couple have moved into the flat above mine, and I find that I am being woken with a start in the middle of the night by their bloodcurdling screams and shouts. I feel it would start our relationship off on a bad footing if I were to say something. It would also be embarrassing to have to go on meeting on the staircase every day for the rest of our lives after such a conversation. The only other person in the house is an old lady on the ground floor who is deaf.

K.W., Ann Street, Edinburgh

A I SUGGEST you enlist the help of a co-operative friend who would be prepared to respond to a telephone call from you, at whatever stage of the day or night, by ringing up the couple in question. Purporting to be a neighbour living further along the street, or even behind your own house, he could express his anger at the annoyance caused, claiming that the noise was 'keeping the whole street awake'. By doing this you can avoid any rancour which might attach itself to you, were you to make the complaint yourself.

Non-stop Socialising

Q I RECENTLY went to stay the weekend with old
friends in the country whom I do not see nearly
enough. On my arrival on Saturday I was told I'd been
asked to drinks before Sunday lunch with a neighbour.
I immediately expressed horror at the thought of having
to make polite conversation on a Sunday morning. Then,
to make matters worse, at breakfast on Sunday I was told
we had all been asked to tea at the house of a particularly
strident woman and her husband. Since I'd already had
to endure their company at dinner on the Saturday, I
visibly balked over my coffee. I felt I'd made the effort
to go to the country to see my friends, not to fraternise
with the local grandees. What tactful excuses should I
have thought up to gracefully decline the morning drinks
and afternoon tea?

Name and address withheld.

A THERE WOULD have been no point in your declin-
ing these invitations since your weekend hosts were
going anyway and you would thereby have seen even
less of them. One of the things that friendship is based
on is the discussion of mutual acquaintances and, no
doubt, your hosts felt at the back of their minds that
these outings would only have served to intensify your
own friendship as you 'bitched' about the people afterwards. When planning future visits to these friends, however, you might pre-empt excessive socialising by saying,
'I'd so love to come and spend a quiet weekend with you
in the country – I've been having such an exhausting
time that it will be bliss not to have to socialise.'

Noses (I)

Q I RECENTLY had lunch with someone who I was hoping would give me a job. I was disconcerted all the way through the lunch by the fact that this person's nose appeared to have bled earlier in the day – there were speckles of blood still on the end of it. I feel sure that my failure to say something led to my being rejected for the position. She would have been embarrassed to see her nose next time she went to the loo, and to have realised that I must have seen it too. But how can you mention such a thing to someone you don't know very well?

C.N., Audley End

A I FIND THE following solution useful for dealing with such problems. Always be ready to speak promptly the moment you have noticed any form of nasal detritus. Say pleasantly, 'Oh, you've been sniffing lilies – you've got pollen on the end of your nose. How lovely!' Anyone with any intelligence will make straight for a mirror and gratefully remove such waste. They will be thrilled that you thought it was pollen and only too eager to push from their minds the suspicion that you were perfectly aware of its genuine composition.

Noses (II)

Q I HAVE ALWAYS found anything to do with noses disgusting. I adore children but cannot understand why their noses have to be running all the time. I usually bring tissues when I go to visit friends with children and simply wipe their noses for them so I can bear to look at them. However, I have one friend in particular whose three children's noses seem to be permanently caked with undislodgeable matter. What should I do as I am shortly to pay a visit there?

L.G., Ludgershall

A MOST TOY shops sell Sir Roy Strong-style false faces comprising glasses, nose and moustache. Why not make a purchase of a set of three false faces – costing only about £1.50 – and request that your friends' children wear the false faces for the duration of your visit. In this way the entire offending nose areas will be screened from your view.

Open Letters, the Acceptability of

Q OUR FAMILY has moved to Tuscany for a year,
possibly more. We want to write to our friends (of
whom we have an incredible number) but find that we
want to say the same thing to all of them – i.e. about
how we are settling in, what schools the children are at,
what our social life is, etc. Is it socially acceptable to
send the same roneoed or photocopied open letter to
everyone, individually addressed of course?

Name withheld, Siena

A NO. RECIPIENTS of such letters are usually resentful. It is galling when a friend presumes you are
mentally interchangeable with a whole herd of other
people. The best procedure would be to write a highly
personalised letter to one close friend 'X', giving all the
details you mention. You may then attach a photocopy
of this letter to the notes that you will scrawl to all your
other friends, explaining that you have tendonitis or
repetitive strain injury and, until such time as you can
write to them properly, you are enclosing a photocopy
of a letter to X 'which has all the news'.

Peacock Noise Pollution

Q OUR SMALL country house in a quiet valley is assailed by the raucous screeching of peacocks. Some difficult neighbours have brought them in to dignify their designer garden. Roosters crowing at dawn are one thing; unnerving foreign screams from peacocks on top of the chimney at four in the morning are quite another. The awful noises continue intermittently throughout the day. Neighbourhood petitions have been ignored. The county authorities are 'investigating' but after a year no action has been taken. We're desperate. What can we do short of a shotgun?

J.D., London SW13

A A FORMER peacock owner of my acquaintance has offered the following solution. Persuade a local grandee – not too local – to buy some peacocks. If necessary, make him a present of a pair. Peacocks are notoriously snobbish and are known to prefer grand houses where there are more pilasters to emerge screeching from behind and more mature trees in which to perch at great height. In no time your neighbours' peacocks will be attracted by the distant screeching from up to five miles away and will fly off to see what is going on. Having found the conditions at the grand house to be superior to their own in the designer garden, they will be loath to return home. Recapture will be pointless as the birds will fly straight back each time.

Place à Table

Q I DO FEEL it is rather pompous and middle-aged
to have placement cards at dinner, but when there
are more than ten people all braying at the top of their
voices as I attempt to seat them I tend to become flustered and forget who is going where. What do other
young marrieds do?

V. de L., London SW12

A WHY NOT take your cue from Lady Alexandra
Elletson, who often serves cold soup as a first course
and, using a pipette creamer, traces the initials of the
guest in question in each bowl.

Plastic People

Q AT A dinner party recently a not so close acquaintance of mine amused us all with a somewhat ribald
attack on cosmetic surgery, particularly the practices of
liposuction and breast implantation. Coincidentally,
only a few weeks before in my doctor's waiting-room,
I had happened upon an extremely out-of-date colour
supplement in which there was one of those 'Where Are
They Now?' features, and in a group photograph of the
Oxford undergraduates there depicted I espied my
acquaintance, 20 years younger but, to my surprise,

sporting a nose of robust proportion and shape. Her present appendage is a shadow of its former self and most delicately modelled. With that dinner party in mind, I feel that a mild riposte is called for. Can you suggest a means?

M.C.Mc.L., London SW10

A DO YOU have any friends in the media? Even on the local paper? Glossy magazines and women's page editors of newspapers are always running articles on cosmetic surgery and always seeking to illustrate them with before and after photographs of people whose noses have been successfully remodelled. Put forward the name and phone number of the person you mention as someone who has had transformation surgery and may be willing to be included in such an article. Your acquaintance will soon be horrified to receive a telephone call from the publication requesting an interview. 'How did you get my name?' she is bound to ask of her would-be exposer. 'Why, M.C.Mc.L suggested I try you,' the journalist should reply. 'She told me she would never have recognised you from an old "Where Are They Now?" feature she saw in her doctor's waiting-room, had not your name been underneath it.'

Predicto-babble

Q CAN YOU recommend any amusing new party games to play around the dinner table? Things are rather dull and predictable in our neck of the woods.

C.H., Stockport

A WHY NOT try out the new game 'Predicto-babble'? Each member of a dinner party lays bets before dinner on the topics of conversation which will be covered by each of those guests at least one place away from him or her (to avoid cheating). Given a plan of the *place à table*, they decide what topics Miss X and Mr Y are most and least likely to cover and what topics Mr W and Miss X are most and least likely to cover. Though many guests begin by determining not to cover the topics that they feel others may feel they are most likely to, they usually, by the second course and the fourth glass of wine, lapse into an all too great predictability. In this way many laughs can be had and money can be made. Also gentle insults can be levelled with impunity.

Presents for People Who Genuinely Do Have Everything

Q CAN YOU suggest a Christmas present for someone who genuinely does have everything?
S.B., Kennington SE11

A YES. AN amusing new product called Maidcall is available from the firm Aidcall which supplies granny alarms. Maidcall is a slim black box the size and shape of a calculator. By discreetly depressing a button on this portable device, staff can be alerted by bleep to attend to their employers' needs at the dinner table or even tennis court – anywhere, in fact, up to 100 metres away. The receiver, which is not portable, is plugged into a wall socket in the quarters where the aides may be waiting for their summons – a summons which has the advantage of being silent from the transmission end and virtually unobservable. The device, costing roughly £500 in a silver case from Asprey's, is already in service in certain ducal households. A cheaper version of the Maidcall (without the silver case) is available for around £150 direct from Aidcall, 363 Fulham Road, SW10 (071 352 2822), and can be put to good use by girls suffering from sexual harassment at work, as colleagues can be discreetly summoned to appear, as though by coincidence, each time molestation seems likely to begin.

Presents for the Kitchen

Q CAN YOU recommend a new kitchen gadget as a Christmas present for a friend who loves cooking but seems already to have everything? Is there anything new on the market?

R.R., London W11

A YES. WHY not buy a pair of snorkling goggles for your friend? He or she can use them while chopping onions, to minimise the flowing streams of tears which afflict many cooks during this process.

Presents for the kitchen

Pretentiousness in Pronunciation

Q HOW SHOULD I pronounce the surname Cecil, when referring to members of that family in conversation? I feel it is a bit of an affectation for me to say 'Sissil' when I hardly know any of them. Yet I would not like others to think that I did not know that 'Sissil' was the correct pronunciation and pull me up on it. I had the same trouble with 'Althrup' before he succeeded.

R.A., w8

A WHY NOT sneeze each time you are pronouncing the surname? In this way people will think that it was just fortuitous that you pronounced it correctly. (You should never let yourself be tricked into saying 'Sissil' Beaton.) Incidentally, the actor Jonathan Cecil uses the phonetic form, as do many friends of the glamorous Lord Michael Cecil.

Prompt Pudding, a

Q CAN YOU recommend a simple, cheap but palate-cleansing dish which I can serve as a pudding course when guests come to supper?

C. de S., NI

A YES. BAKED banana is currently acceptable. Simply pop the banana into the oven in its skin and ten minutes later remove it, when it has gone black. Guests can enjoy the satisfying sensation of peeling the black banana skin off to reveal the still yellow contents. They can then ingest it with Greek yoghurt served as a supplement.

Punishing Suppliers of 'Bought' Cakes

Q THIS YEAR I opened our garden to the public in aid of our local church roof. Various ladies were asked to bake cakes to be sold on the day and they did so. Unfortunately I have since heard that some of the cakes we sold as 'Fresh Home-baked Cakes' were, in fact, shop-bought and past their sell-by-dates with the wrappers taken off. How can I prevent this from happening again next year? Obviously we cannot taste the cakes before offering them for sale.

Name and address withheld

A WOULD IT be possible for you to write to all the ladies involved instead of asking them verbally if they might be persuaded to provide cakes? This would afford you the opportunity to include in your letter the following piece of Euroese: 'I am obliged by law to mention that due to new EC regulations all cakes to be sold as fresh and home-baked must legally fulfil these requirements, or their supplier will stand liable to prosecution and a term of imprisonment.'

RAC Men

Q ON MORE than one occasion this year my husband and I have had to call in the RAC Rescue Service. My husband knows nothing about car engines yet insists on putting his head in the bonnet alongside the mechanic and feigning interest and knowledge about what might be wrong. Do you not think that he should just let the man get on with it, without pretending to a knowledge he quite obviously does not have?

R.R., Burton-on-the-Water

A NO. MANY RAC men derive great satisfaction from assisting members of the public who have been disabled by their lack of knowledge or car maintenance skills. They take great pleasure in the personalities they meet while going about their business and enjoy the interaction that the job affords them.

Recovering Borrowed Books

Q I HAVE AN extremely good library and a reasonably active social life. This means that people staying in the house frequently begin a book and then want to take it with them when they leave. They always promise to return the book when they have finished reading it, but my experience is that people invariably forget to do so. How can I best deter such borrowers?

L.G, Ludgershall

A WHY NOT take your cue from the late bibliophile and poet Lord Moyne whose bookshelves were dentilled by pieces of stiff card? These stood in place of books on loan and on them borrowers were invited to fill out their name, the book's name, and the date on which it was borrowed.

The ritual of writing out these details tends to instill a sense of responsibility on the part of borrowers. They will return finished books with alacrity as they will not wish subsequent house-guests to see their unreliability advertised by the date-stamped cards.

Restaurants: Avoiding the Bill

Q WHAT DO you do when a friend whom you have arranged to take out to dinner goes and asks two other people to join you in the restaurant? It is not that my husband and I dislike the other two people – just that we do not wish to have to pay for them. Our friend, who is still earning 'funny money' in Tokyo, is not tuned in to the general climate of penny-pinching in Britain. As he is in town for three nights only, he obviously wants to see as many people as possible and embarrassment over payment will not have occurred to him. I cannot cook at home because I am working till 8 o'clock on the night in question. What should I do?

J.S., WI

A PUT THE following plan into action. Stage one: you arrive at the restaurant first and greet the two extra guests with excessive enthusiasm. Say that your husband will be so thrilled to see them – it will be a surprise for him because you simply haven't had time to mention that they were coming along. If you have already admitted that your husband knows they are coming, then ignore this stage of the plan. Stage two: your husband bursts through the door looking flustered but good-natured. Greeting the two extras with feigned surprise but genuine enthusiasm, he calms down slightly and explains that he is late because he has locked his wallet into the boot of his car (or someone else's car) and that it cannot be retrieved till tomorrow. 'But,' he cries, childishly waving a handful of notes, 'X owed me some money so I dropped in on him on the way here.' It can then turn out that the amount of money X was able to pay back was commensurate only with the cost of three dinners not five. This will allow your friend from Tokyo to pay the difference, were he not already intending to do so.

Reusing Stamps

Q I RECEIVED a number of Christmas cards over the past few weeks whose envelopes bear stamps which seem to have escaped the attention of a post office franking machine. What is the position about my reusing these stamps on another envelope?

A.B., w8

A THE OFFENCE you are considering is punishable by up to 14 years' imprisonment under Section 13 of the 1891 Stamp Duties Management Act. I strongly advise against your taking the risk of being apprehended in the course of trying to make such a saving.

Schoolboy Blackmailers

Q A SCHOOL-TEACHER colleague recently attended a Chippendales' 'concert' organised as an end-of-term outing by a female member of the school staff, a physical education teacher who is a militant feminist and (inexplicably) a member of her village Women's Institute. She led my colleague to believe that the Chippendales were a troupe of light entertainers, offering a genteel evening of 18th-century music and dance. She claimed later, unconvincingly to my mind, to have been confused by the Chippendale label and its connotation with the renowned 18th-century furniture designer. Imagine my colleague's distress on finding herself trapped one Saturday night in the front row of a packed dance hall of dubious repute, staring at a male strip show of unrestrained lewdness and vulgarity. Somehow, though, she managed to endure three hours of this entertainment, but towards the close two terrible events occurred. Intoxicated by the feverish atmosphere, my colleague foolishly allowed herself to respond to the performers' seductive cries for volunteers to assist them with their garish climax. Thus, throwing all caution – and an undergarment – to the wind, she fatally mounted the stage. Now the second terrible event occurred. Locked in the bronzed arms of a loin-clothed Chippendale, she tore her gaze from his to look down into the crowded auditorium. To her apoplectic consternation, she now found herself staring into the camera lens of a particularly abhorrent and troublesome boy from her school. (This boy was recently expelled from the Scouts for some undisclosed offence.) My colleague fears blackmail. She believes the boy may approach the tabloids with his photograph. Already she has encountered him loitering outside her classroom, ostentatiously reading the *Sun* newspaper. She interprets this as a veiled threat. My colleague urgently needs a convincing story to satisfy parents as to why she was discovered in the early hours, in a seedy, public dance hall, wearing immodest dress and in the embrace of a near naked male. She is also worried that the incident, if it should enter the public domain, may dash her hope of becoming head of her religious studies department. Mary, can you help?

R.B., *West Country*

A YOUR COLLEAGUE should call the boy's bluff by approaching him and asking, 'By any chance did you get some pictures of me the other night? We want them for the school magazine.' She should chuckle as she makes the request and explain that she is trying to put together a fun quiz in the magazine which will show each member of staff in the mode which most contrasts with their true nature and in which they are least likely ever to appear in real life. The pupils will then be asked to identify these teachers in their baffling disguises and there will be a prize of £10 for the winner. 'Someone was taking pictures for me,' she can say, 'but sadly she exposed the film.' Once having gained possession of the prints and negatives, she can destroy them 'accidentally'.

Skinheads

Q MAY I AVAIL myself of your column to pass on a tip to readers? Last Saturday evening when waiting for a tube at Sloane Square station, I was vaguely observing a lone skinhead who was standing on the platform with me. Suddenly he swung round with his teeth bared and asked me what I was looking at. It was a nasty moment but the untruthful answer I gave was inspired. I replied, 'Sorry I was staring but you are the complete spitting image of my son Derek who is also a skinhead.' The youth's aggression just melted away, he even seemed to smile at me. I hope your readers may find my experience useful.

R. B. K., St John's Wood

A THANK YOU for passing on your tip which readers may indeed find useful when answering similar queries from Hell's Angels, football fans and other types, though in my experience skinheads are like piranha fish. They only attack in groups.

Smelling House-guests

Q I HAVE AN elderly bachelor aesthete coming to stay for Christmas. He is extremely good value but can also be rather sharp and touchy. For this reason I feel I cannot risk being frank with him about his clothes, of which he has one set, and which smell appalling. (He lives in Norfolk so tends to sleep in them during the winter.) What should I do?

V.M., London WII

A INVITE YOUR guest to sit in the kitchen while you make some large, custard-based confection for consumption over Christmas. This will enable you to 'accidentally' spill a good pint or so of milk over the clothes, which you can then insist on stripping off him. Have to hand a spare outfit of men's clothing in his size which he can wear until you have effected the cleaning process on the offensive set.

Smoking Irritants

Q WHAT CAN one do to stop old friends, whom one values, from smoking between courses when they come to dinner? My wife and I are non-smokers and I am, besides, bronchitic. They know we don't like their smoking, but if they abstain for our sake there is a sense of strain and a danger that we and they may become socially incompatible. It is all right out of doors, of course, but we don't like to shoo them out each time they light up.

J.D.P., Alton, Hants

A INSTALL smoke alarms just above your dining table and in all reception rooms. These usually come ready-fitted with 'suckers' so that they can be stuck on at random around the house without recourse to workmen. When friends have their first puff on their first cigarette sirens will sound and you can apologise: 'Gosh, I am sorry. Shall we all move into the garden while you smoke?' The nuisance of having to go into the garden each time will encourage your friends to moderate their addiction accordingly.

Social Nudity

Q I HAVE RECENTLY become a member of an exclu-
sive health club in the Notting Hill area and would
like to be put right on a point of etiquette. What is the
procedure about meeting people one knows naked in the
ladies' changing-room (or, indeed, letting them see one

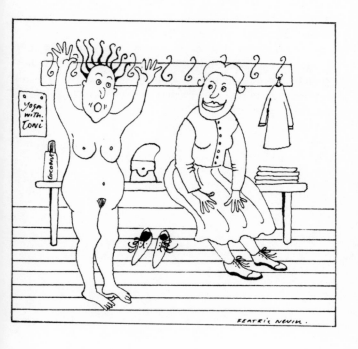

naked)? I find it embarrassing when people such as the owner of the local bookshop or wine bar, whom I have been seeing for 15 years with clothes on, suddenly appear at close quarters in the nude. I am now terrified of seeing Antonia Fraser naked, though so far I have only seen her fully clothed putting on gym shoes. I am on 'hello' terms with Antonia and would not like her to think I was trying to get too familiar.

E.S., WII

A WHILE YOU are in the changing-room it is desirable for you to intersperse your normal movements with peculiar little blinking gestures, as though trying to reposition a contact lens before deciding to remove it entirely. You can also appear to grope for your clothes. Mutter, 'Haw! I can't see a thing', while you do this. Those who are present in the changing-room with you will heave a sigh of relief. If, however, you are addressed by Lady Antonia while one of you is naked, then it is correct for you to go so close to her own face, while replying, as to prevent either of you getting a view of one another's nude bodies.

Spittle

Q WHAT IS THE correct way to remove spittle which someone has accidentally spat onto one's face while talking enthusiastically?

C.S., Islington

A IF ONE HAS been spat on by an old friend, then it is correct to cry, 'Ugh! Stop spitting!' before openly removing the effluvium with an exaggerated dabbing action. Should your interlocutor be less well known to you, you can avoid embarrassment by pretending not to have noticed for a few seconds and continuing your conversation. You should then drop or knock something to the floor. During the stooping and recovery process you will have ample time to discreetly blot the spittle onto some suitable part of your own clothing.

Standing Up

Q I RECENTLY, out of nervousness, stood up for Lord Michael Pratt when having drinks before luncheon in a private house. As I am a woman, I presume this was incorrect. What is the correct protocol about whom one stands up for in a private house and should one take one's cue from one's hostess or not?

Name withheld

A IT IS BEST to be prepared for any eventuality by pretending that you enjoy standing anyway in the run-up to such luncheons when people are assembling in staggered groups. You can pretend to admire paintings or views until such moment as luncheon is served. Alternatively, you can pretend to be so engrossed in conversation with someone that you have not noticed a new arrival in the room until you are sure what the others present are doing.

Stopping People from Probing One's Bachelor Status

Q I AM A 34-year-old bachelor. Because I am supposed to be eligible, I am always being asked by women I meet at dinner and drinks parties if I am married and if not why not. I do not know the answer to this, nor am I that keen on being drawn into discussion of the subject with someone I have just met – though I realise the question is often posed flirtatiously. How can I swiftly close the subject without seeming rude?

N.S., WII

A IN THE MORE casual and ephemeral atmosphere of a drinks party you could answer the question 'Are you married?' with an enigmatic but conclusive 'Not exactly.' At a dinner party it would be safer to allow an emotional rigour to come over your face before you whisper the answer, 'Ask me that question again in three months' time.' You can continue giving this reply *ad nauseam* should you happen to run into the same questioner again.

Suitable Shopping Bags for Males

Q I AM A 50-year-old divorced male who has recently
moved to Aldeburgh. What is the least effeminate
shopping bag to carry when making purchases in the
high street?

N.H., Aldeburgh

A THE IDEAL shopping basket for a heterosexual
male to carry is a deep Kenyan straw basket or
kikapou. As it is rugged in appearance, it is an acceptable
load-bearer and will give no grounds for confusion to
your new neighbours.

Sunday Papers

Q HOW CAN I tell whether or not I have already read
a certain Sunday paper? I often find myself halfway
through a paper before I recognise something I have
read before and realise I have already read that whole
paper once. We tend to have a lot of people around at
the weekend, so it is impossible to keep track of what
one has already read by stacking up a pile.

S.H., Moreton-in-Marsh

A WHY NOT keep a red crayon handy and strike a diagonal mark through the front page of each paper you have read?

Swearing

Q I AM GOING to stay with relations of my husband's for Christmas. The problem is that my husband has got into the habit of using the 'f' word as an adjective. He has picked this up from friends in racing circles in which we have been spending an increasing amount of time this year. 'Pass me the f—ing newspaper, would you, darling?' 'I'm just going to have a quick f—ing bath.' 'What time will we be f—ing arriving at?' etc. He is almost unaware that he is doing it. I am worried that my in-laws may think that this new habit is something that I have introduced him to or even that I condone it. Yet how can I curb his tongue over the Christmas period without being a complete bore and saying, 'Darling! Stop swearing!' after each sentence he utters?

S.M., Tisbury, Wilts

A TELL YOUR husband, in front of his relations, that you are going to start fining him £1 for each expletive uttered over the Christmas period. The money can go to the Injured Jockeys Fund. Then, each time he swears in front of you, you can cry 'Ding!' and follow it with a girlish and pleasant laugh. Explain that 'Ding!' is meant to represent the sound of a coin tinkling into a tin bucket. The huge irritation you will cause him by saying 'Ding!' after virtually every sentence he speaks will no doubt bring him swiftly to his senses.

Table Manners

Q MY BOYFRIEND, to whom I am engaged, has many desirable qualities. However he has one major defect which I cannot ignore. He eats with his mouth open and talks with the food visibly swirling around inside as though it were a concrete mixer. There is no problem when we are alone together as I simply lean forward and snap his jaw shut. He responds unaggressively. However, when we are at very big dinner parties, I am often too far away to attract his attention. What can I do, as I otherwise squirm with embarrassment on his behalf as I see the horrified expression on the face of his interlocutor?

R.M., W10

A WHY NOT bring along with you to social engagements a few small boulders of ready mix cement? Each one need only be the size of, say, five peas *in toto*. You can easily find a way of discreetly slipping one of these mini-boulders on to your boyfriend's plate – perhaps placing it immediately adjacent to his pile of salt. This means that each time he loads his fork and directs it towards the flavour-enhancing salt, his attention will be attracted by the mini-boulder. This will remind him to try and correct his defect by keeping his mouth shut.

Talking to Oneself: Being Caught

Q WHEN I HAVE a hangover I am often consumed by guilt and am quite beastly to myself. Especially when driving alone in the car, I can't help cussing my stupid behaviour of the night before and sometimes slap myself across the forehead. Occasionally pulling up at traffic lights, I realise I have been caught unawares by other motorists. Should I shake my head and pretend that I was just singing along with the music or return their stare as if it's them that's completely barking?

D.R., St John of God's, Lucan

A NEITHER method is correct. You should continue to talk to yourself but glance backwards and downwards at the same time. This will give the impression that you have been addressing a companion who is lying down in the rear passenger seat – perhaps also hungover, but outside the field of vision of your observers.

Taxis

Q ALTHOUGH it is an extravagance, I always consider taking taxis to be worth the relatively minimal outlay. Those moments of complete mental freedom in that capsule of carelessness always seem to me to pay for themselves. One thing I find rather mean about taxi drivers, however, is the way they keep the meter running after you have arrived at your destination so that by the time I personally have gathered together all my bits and pieces, the meter has usually clicked on another 40 or so pence. Is it reasonable to say to the driver, 'You can turn off the meter now,' when arriving at one's destination?

N.C., WI

A NO. A BETTER method is to screw up your eyes on arrival at the destination and shout, 'Thank you. How much is that? I'm very short-sighted.' You can then grapple around for your bits and pieces for as long as necessary before dismounting from the cab and the *prix* will be *fixe*.

The Foreign Secretary Writes

Q EARLIER THIS year I led a group of three EC foreign ministers and a European commissioner on a visit to South Africa. We flew overnight in a plane in which the RAF had kindly put beds. As we finished a nightcap, I wondered whether I should wait for my guests to realise they should start to make the most of the few hours' flight, and move off to their bunks, as they would if house guests. Or should I lead the way and risk accusations of the host breaking up the party?

D. Hurd, Foreign and Commonwealth Office, London SWI

A DESPITE initial resentment, most people are usually grateful to find themselves tucked up in bed, when they might otherwise have been staying up and undermining their health. A tactful way of bossing your fellow ministers into their bunks would have been for you discreetly to ask the pilot to dim the lights in the cabin – or even to flash them on and off as on commercial premises. You could have then stood up, with a sign of reluctance, and said, 'Oh dear, I'm afraid this happens. We have to go to our beds now,' as though it were an RAF custom.

The Hons.

Q MY FATHER has recently been made a life peer and I am wondering how I can best take advantage of my own new status as 'The Hon.'. I understand it is wrong for me to be addressed as The Hon. anywhere except on an envelope and I find this rather depressing. Can you advise me on how to exploit the title more fully?
Name withheld, London

A YOU CAN ask your bank to put 'The Hon.' on your cheque book. This is quite legitimate as it is in fact part of your official name now. You can always claim that 'the bank did it themselves' as many banks, such as Coutts, genuinely do take this initiative. However, you can best announce your new status to the world by sitting on a committee for some charity ball or similar. You can then send out hundreds of letters to friends and acquaintances which will advise them to write to 'The Hon. X X' with their donations or cheques for the purchase of tickets. Many 'Hons' have postcards printed headed 'From The Hon. So and So' and you, too, can have this done on the pretext that you needed a quantity to facilitate the speedy reply to your charity correspondence.

The Telephone:
Catching Your Wife Out

Q I OFTEN COME in and find my wife yattering on the telephone to her friend who lives 50 miles away. This is always at peak time and when she really should be getting on with other things. I bitterly resent the waste of money and time but she always hisses, '*She* rang *me*.' How can I check up on who really rang whom?

A.M., Fonthill

A NEXT TIME your wife says '*She* rang *me*' you can check the veracity of her claim by marching straight to the telephone and clicking down the receiver buttons with your fingers. If, when you release them, the line has gone dead, then you will have exposed your wife in her deception.

Tickling and Teasing

Q I HAVE OFTEN felt frustrated on visits to hair-dressing salons as I find my submission to the sensuous relief of being given digitocranial teasing is usually thwarted by having to make small talk to the hairdresser. I am a well known public figure and do not wish to seem unfriendly. What do you advise?

I.G., SW1

A WHY NOT patronise a Japanese salon? At most of those in London's Brook Street, full dorsal and cranial relief (in the form of shiatsu massage) form a natural part of even the most straightforward wash and blow-dry. There is no need for you to make small talk with the hairdressers of such establishments. They prefer to concentrate on the geisha-like promotion of complete relaxation. More to the point you will not run the risk of being photographed by paparazzi as you leave.

Tip on Bet-hedging, a

Q MAY I PASS on a solution to your readers? I was recently pressed to make a decision about a certain social invitation by a certain time of day and agreed that I would do so, but when that time came round I was not ready to give my answer. Basically I was bet-hedging and trying to decide which of two invitations I had for the night in question would be the better one. Meanwhile the call was about to come through and I knew I had to say yes or no. So what did I do? Speaking in a high-pitched and unnatural voice, I recorded the following message into my answerphone: 'Sorry. All lines to the Carmarthen exchange are temporarily out of service. Please try later.' With the aid of a tape-recorder, I was able to make this message come continuously out of the outgoing message tape. It worked a treat. Neither hostess suspected a thing and I was able to make the (correct) decision at leisure.

A THANK YOU very much for taking the trouble to pass this tip on to other *Spectator* readers.

Truth with Tact

Q HOW CAN I reply effectively to those unnecessary remarks, 'You must come round for a meal some time,' and 'You haven't been round to see us for ages,' when their very use confirms that neither party has much in common with the other?

R.C.A., Marchamley, Shrewsbury

A REPLY AMBIGUOUSLY, 'Yes, why don't we arrange something?' before changing the subject. If pushed, then suggest, 'We've shot some wonderful film of autumn colour. There are four hours of it so maybe we should come one evening at about six so we could watch it for two hours before supper and then finish watching it after supper. Do ring when you feel like seeing it.'

Unpalatable Fudge

Q MY WIFE MAKES a most unpalatable fudge which she offers to guests, urging them to spoil themselves and take several pieces. For their ensuing discomfort my only remedy has been to offer the use of an ashtray or napkin, but this is messy and does little to improve the atmosphere. My wife is a proud woman and does not take kindly to criticism. Is there a way out?

R.H.D., London NW3

A FUDGE IS a simple dish to make – indeed it is often made by children in nursery school as a play activity. Quickly run some up yourself – of a similar colour to that presented by your wife – and discreetly substitute it for the mixture she supplies.

Unsuitable Gifts

Q EACH CHRISTMAS and birthday my *belle-mère* gives
presents like special German cleansing agents,
books bought at a bazaar, various small kitchen gadgets
– essentially totally inappropriate things which I neither
want nor need. To make matters worse, when I politely
say 'Thank you for the lovely present!' with feigned
enthusiasm, she replies, 'Oh, they weren't lovely. They
were awful!' I long to say, 'Yes, they were awful. Why
then did you give them to me?' but I feel this would be
going too far. What should I do?

A.S., Glos

A MOST PEOPLE in the upper-middle classes have
drawers full of dud gifts which they have bought
at bazaars and agricultural shows in a bid to be both
charitable and efficient. Reply to your mother-in-law's
Exocets by sending your own Scuds. Set up a dud present
drawer of your own. Give her presents like a Danish/
English dictionary, a bicycle lock if she does not have a
bicycle. What about a jewelled cat collar if she does not
have a cat? The ultimate deterrent might be a 'willy-
warmer', a knitted object in the shape of a cigar which
is meant to be humorous and can be purchased in expen-
sive joke shops. If your mother-in-law questions your
choice you can reply blandly, 'Yes, isn't it terrible? I buy
all these things throughout the year and then feel I have
to give them to people whether they are suitable or not.
Don't you? Let's have a pact in future and only give each
other things we know we really need.'

Unwelcome Intimacy

Q I WORK IN a heritage interpretation centre. Some of my work consists of showing 'ramblers' an Ordnance Survey map on a table as I point out rights of way and areas of special interest. The detail involved requires their faces and mine to come into very close proximity as we 'pore' over the map. I am worried I may pick up infections and resent the intimacy with total strangers. Post-office and rail-ticket officials have grilles to protect them. What can I do?

R.W., Matlock, Derbyshire

A WHY NOT pick up the whole map when dealing with these total strangers? With a comment like 'Let's shed some light on the situation', you can move to a wall near a window where you can spread the map at above eye level. Your left arm should be stretched out, securing the map against the wall, while your right gesticulates and points out the details. These actions should preclude the intimacy you fear.

Using Full Titles on an Envelope

Q I HAVE TO send a thank-you letter to someone grand who has written very warmly to me about a recent exhibition of my paintings. Do you agree with me that there is something rather flattering in not putting someone's full title on an envelope and that to put a more casual address implies a closer and more intimate friendship? I feel that to get the full title fully correct would indicate a rather creepy knowledge of etiquette or that I had been looking the person in question up in a handbook. Then I wonder if one should get the title slightly wrong to cover up one's creepiness? It is only that I am trying to be more personal. What do you think?

Name and address withheld

A BY ALL MEANS continue to address the person in question in the manner in which you have been accustomed in conversation inside the envelope. On the envelope, however, you must stick rigidly to the formal rules of address. Not to do so could undermine your correspondent's authority with his or her postman or staff.

Vicars Dropping In

Q WHAT CAN one do when vicars drop in to see one without ringing first? The other day I was just settling down to chat with an old friend, whom I had not seen for over a year, when the door-bell rang and there was the new young curate who has just joined our parish. The result was a one-and-a-quarter-hour-long ordeal in

which the three of us made very sticky conversation and we had to drink tea instead of gin. What should I have said?

B.B., County Antrim

A I FIND THE simplest way of deflecting vicars until a later, more convenient time is to greet them warmly, but say, 'What a pity I didn't know you were coming. I've just taken my medication.' You need explain no further. Let the vicar make his own assumptions as to whether you have taken sleeping pills, broncho-dilators or even laxatives. You can then issue an invitation for him to visit again at a precise date in the future.

Wedding Presents

Q HOW CAN I most tactfully establish whether a close friend has actually given me a wedding present or not? We got married six weeks ago but, as far as I know, there has been nothing from this particular person though she attended the wedding and we have seen her since. I don't mind whether she has given me one or not but the trouble is that she is rather mean and may not have. On the other hand, she *might* have given me one which has been mislaid and be wondering why I have been so rude in not thanking her for it. What should I do?

S.P., EI

A ASK A MUTUAL friend to serve as go-between and, during casual conversation, suddenly interject, 'Oh damn! I've got to buy a wedding present . . . have you any ideas? What did *you* give S.P.?' The suspect can then reply either, 'Nothing. Quite honestly I can't afford to buy wedding presents', or, 'An incredible lamp from Conran. But she hasn't thanked me for it.' Your mutual friend can pass on her findings.

When Parents-in-law Serve Disgusting Food

Q MY HUSBAND and I go about once a month to stay with his parents in Bath. My problem is that though I enjoy every other aspect of our visits there, I cannot eat my mother-in-law's cooking. She is rather old and tends to favour austerity dishes such as tripe and spam. When she 'cooks' a fish finger she does it by putting a frozen one into a slow Aga for just long enough so that it thaws and is warm but still cold in the centre. What can I do? We already have to bring drink and keep it in our room but it would be too complicated to bring food as well.

C.C., Worcs.

A THE IDEAL solution to this problem is that you should pretend to have become a vegetarian. Vegetables cannot be made disgusting in quite the same way as meat and most people could manage to put up with eating only vegetables for a weekend with equanimity.

Which God-daughter?

❦

Q I HAVE TWO young nieces, the Misses Phipps, who have been living abroad for the last three years. I attended both of their christenings, which took place about four and six years ago, and am godfather to one of them. Unfortunately, I cannot remember which one I am godfather to. I have tried asking others who might remember, but no one can. Now that the family is returning to this country, how do I find out which niece is my god-daughter without alerting the parents to my plight?

Name and address withheld

A WRITE A LETTER which opens, 'My dear god-daughter,' and then goes on to ask whether she would like a certain 'Little Pony' or other likely present which you have seen in an English shop. Address the envelope in fountain pen, say, to 'Miss J Phipps'. Then smudge the 'J' as though by rainwater so that it is unrecognisable as any initial at all. Your god-daughter's parents will intercept the letter and will reply on her behalf. 'Sarah would love the "Little Pony"', for example. Alternatively, the little girl may scratch out her own reply, if she is able to write, and will no doubt sign off with her own name, which she will be more likely to use than 'your loving god-daughter'.

Working Off Dullards

Q HAVE YOU any suggestions for ways in which one can repay hospitality and debts of friendship to people who, regrettably, one finds too dull to invite to dinner or on holiday?

A.C., w8

A INDEED. Now that so much of social life revolves around the raising of sums for charity this affords a hostess the perfect opportunity to work off dullards. Simply buy some tickets to a concert or play which is being staged in aid of charity and there will be no need for you to spend any time in conversation with your worthy friends. No doubt, they too will enjoy an evening more where they are under no obligations to be amusing.

Yawning

Q MY HUSBAND does something which I find fantastically annoying each morning, which is that he yawns and then emits a high-pitched woman's scream at the end of the yawn. I tend to be bad-tempered first thing in the morning but I think I could find this annoying anyway as one doesn't want to think one has married another woman. How can I stop him? He says he can't help it.

Name and address withheld

A IT IS ALWAYS best to treat these sort of offences in the homeopathic manner – like with like. Next time your husband yawns in a woman's voice why don't you yawn back in a low-pitched growl to counter him? No doubt he will find it shocking to hear a deep male voice coming from his wife's body and in this way you may cure him of his irritating quirk.